Discovering the Champion Inside of You

Alex Grant Jr.

Copyright © 2014 by Alex Grant Jr.

Discovering the Champion Inside of You
by Alex Grant Jr.

Printed in the United States of America

Edited by Xulon Press

ISBN 9781498415279

All rights reserved solely by the author. The author guarantees all contents are original and do not infringe upon the legal rights of any other person or work. No part of this book may be reproduced in any form without the permission of the author. The views expressed in this book are not necessarily those of the publisher.

Scripture quotations taken from the King James Version (KJV) – *public domain*

www.xulonpress.com

Mother Hines
Love you with Everything
In Me
Best wishes
Alex M Brt
11/20/14

DEDICATION

This book is dedicated to the Holy Spirit: thank you for using me as a vessel to encourage people to go after their dreams and not allowing anything to stop them from achieving their purpose in life.

To my parents Alexander and Eliza Grant; to my wife Mary; my children—Trey, Taylor, Tierra, and Jeffrey; and my siblings Darnell and Angela: thank you for your support and understanding; all of the encouragement, patience, and faith that you had in me.

To my BCM Church family: God has blessed me with a great support group!

To Kenneth Gibbons Sr. who kept after me to write of my experiences and share with the world: thank you.

To Dr. Delphine Riley-Poteat, Apostle: Thank you for allowing the Lord to use you mightily in calling forth this assignment in my life.

And, finally, to my cousin Joseph Baxter Jr.: thanks for your wisdom, insight, and encouragement.

Contents

Foreword ix
Introduction.. xiii
1] The Path 17
2] Stay Focused.. 27
3] Activating Our Faith 39
4] Just Do You 51
5] Understanding the Transitional stage 59
6] Submission... 69
7] Launch Into The Deep 81
8] Preparing to take off 95
9] Thinking Outside the Box 109
10] Stretching for the finish line 125
Epilogue... 137

Foreword

"Inspiring book. Pastor Alexander Grant inspires God's people to accept, follow, flow in, and fulfill the Creator's plans for their lives. You will be enlightened on how to handle life's challenges by turning them into opportunities to go where many men only dream of. Every Christian must know who they are and who they are not. Wrong identity brings wasted potentials and vision. This book provides information on how to discover your purpose. It contains practical solutions and strategies to help you to discover who you really are and how to unleash your unique potentials. Don't wait to start your journey tomorrow, but start now."

Dr. Michael D. Gadsden, Sr., PhD
Presiding Bishop of New Vision Outreach
Ministries International Fellowship, Savannah, Georgia

"Truly Pastor Alexander Grant really allowed the Holy Spirit to speak to his soul. This book is very inspiring to me."

Dr. C. H. Brown
Senior Pastor of True Word Full Gospel Baptist Church
North Charleston, North Carolina

"Often times in life, it is necessary for Christian and non-Christians alike to be reminded of their God-given purpose. Certainly God has given predestined our end, but getting there can be complicated to understand. Bishop Alex Grant has given us practical tools for the journey, making it easier to comprehend and obtain. Remember there is a journey we are on, but the journey is not the destination. Thank you Bishop, I am ready to keep walking with the tools you have given."

Bishop Marc L. Neal
Dominion Family Church
Come Alive Ministry International Fellowship, Akron, Ohio

"Discovering the Champion Inside of You" is a powerful narrative of your God-given purpose. Everyone is a winner, if we take the time to look within ourselves and see our personal gifts and talents. Pick up a copy today and discover the real champion in *you*!"

Apostle J. Q. Lockette
Miracle Revival Assemblies
Stone Mountain, Georgia

"Each of us was born with a champion within us, and this book helps the reader discover exactly what God has intended you to triumph and champion over. Alex Grant's compelling and informative style of writing makes this book a must-read."

Apostle Gregory W. Brunson
Church of the Harvest
Rincon, Georgia

"I believe that everyone has a desire deep inside of them to be able to feel good about themselves. However, life's circumstances will sometimes cloud one's ability to believe that this can happen.

Pastor Alexander Grant developed the contents of this book to guide you as you look inside yourself and begin to see what you may not have seen before or what you thought you had lost.

So, I encourage you to read the book thoroughly and, by the grace of God, allow it to lead you to a greater appreciation of who you are and direct you toward who you want to be. After reading this book you will be able to celebrate and appreciate the new person that has always been living inside of you!"

Because of Calvary,

Dr. Delphine Riley-Poteat, Apostle
Kingdom Builders Full Gospel Word and Deliverance Ministries, Inc.
Hardeeville, SC
Yanceyville, NC
Charleston, SC
Liberia, West Africa

INTRODUCTION

A man that works with his hands is a laborer.
A man that works with his hands and brain is a craftsman.
A man that works with his hands and brain and his heart is an artist.

Louis Nizer

My purpose for writing this book is to encourage individuals who may feel discouraged and all alone. My hope is for them is to understand that they are not alone. Many times in life we are faced with troublesome and challenging situations that may cause many of us discomfort and a lot of sleepless nights. My prayers are to inspire you and to expand your vision so that you won't allow the obstacles and the negativity of people to deter and discourage you from finishing your course in life. It is to ignite that fire to your faith so that the supernatural favor of God would increase and manifest in your heart, permitting you to live a complete and fulfilling life; full of all the promises God has ordained for you.

In a study conducted at Taylor University, researchers studied the self-esteem levels of more than 1,500 people, including a number of Evangelical Christians, and found that there was no difference in self-esteem between believers and non-believers. However, there was a significant difference between those that were highly educated and those with fewer educational attainments. This is consistent with other studies that have shown that people who have achieved more in life tend to have a better self-worth attitude than those who have less.

Reading the study provoked me to challenge the saints, on the notion that we have options that the world seems to ignore: In Matthew 11:28–29, Jesus says, "Come to Me, all *you* who labor and are heavy laden, and I will give you rest. Take My yoke upon you and learn from Me, for I am gentle and lowly in heart, and you will find rest for your souls." You see, God wants his children to cast all of their cares upon Him, the one who never sleeps or slumbers. A relationship with God changes trivial, insignificant, and laborious toil into spiritual productivity and purpose. His word serves as a buffer in our lives, which creates distance between the enemy and us. He provides us with the assurance that he will never leave us or forsake us.

When we have a heart after God to please Him, we can take solace in knowing that God states in His word, "No good thing will He withhold from those who walk upright before Him." Even when we are going through challenging times, whether a health crisis, a financial crisis, a bad marriage, a substance abuse storm, the loss of a job, or maybe we have had our savings depleted—whatever our test is, just know that God has that final say and that it's not over until God says that it's over. We will use the adversity in our lives to become the catalyst that will catapult us to our divine purpose, to inspire us and move us to reach into the vast resources that dwell inside of us, enabling us to excel at every level we face.

It's time to get back into the game of life and then take an invested role in the direction of our life again, refusing to settle for average and barely making it. Instead, allow our dreams to take root inside of us and begin producing the harvest that was assigned to our life. Don't let one awkwardly frustrating moment rob us of our potential. We should become all that we can be, reaching for the stars with passion and fervor. This is our season to achieve everything that God has for us. The journey has been too long and tedious to turn back now and quit. Go look in the mirror and see the champion that we are in life, born to succeed and accomplish all the things we put your mind to.

Remember the word of God in Deuteronomy 28:1–6:

> Now it shall come to pass, if you diligently obey the voice of the LORD your God, to observe carefully all His commandments which I command you today, that the LORD your God will set you high above all nations of the earth. And all these blessings shall come upon you and overtake you, because you obey the voice of the LORD your God: Blessed *shall you be* in the city, and blessed *shall you be* in the country. Blessed *shall be* the fruit of your body, the produce of your ground and the increase of your herds, the increase of your cattle and the offspring of your flocks. Blessed *shall be* your basket and your kneading bowl. Blessed *shall you be* when you come in, and blessed *shall you be* when you go out.

God has given us so much instruction and wisdom into how He wants to bless us and be prosperous in our lives. My hope is that this book will serve to motivate, inspire, and encourage us to strive to become all that we can be. No matter what curve balls life tries to throw our way, just remember that we are more than a conqueror.

"And my God shall supply all your need according to His riches in glory by Christ Jesus." -Philippians 4:19

(1)
THE PATH

When we wake up from our confused state of mind, that is enlightenment.

~ *Dzogchen Ponlop*

One of the most rewarding and challenging things in life is reaching the destiny and purpose God has planned for our life. We must effectively and carefully pay close attention and adhere to the words provided by God that direct us in prayer and fellowship with Him.

This alone is very challenging and often frightening knowing that the Almighty himself has a crucial role for us to fulfill and that from the beginning of the awesome foundation of the world, He had us in His plan for a particular purpose and duration of time. Romans 8:29–30 states:

> For whom He foreknew, He also predestined *to be* conformed to the image of His Son, that He might be the firstborn among many brethren. Moreover whom He predestined, these He also called; whom He called, these He also justified; and whom He justified, these He also glorified.

This means our destiny and purpose was already set in motion before we entered this world.

Therefore, our mission must be to seek God for His will and to get a better understanding for our lives, by allowing Him to reveal to us our true identity. Far too many of us go through our various roles in life haphazardly and aimlessly wandering around, sometimes for years, looking to define ourselves, blindly attaching ourselves to people and material things as a surrogate representation of who we really are and meant to be. We seek attention and affirmation from all of the wrong sources, and we tend to measure our self-worth based upon the most asinine things, especially material possessions. We never get a deeper appreciation for what God has for us, sees for us, and wants for us because we're so busy measuring happiness and success with objects and conditions that are really meaningless.

In Matthew 6: 25–27 the Lord says,

> Therefore I say to you, do not worry about your life, what you will eat or what you will drink; nor about your body, what you will put on. Is not life more than food and the body more than clothing? Look at the birds of the air, for they neither sow nor reap nor gather into barns; yet your heavenly Father feeds them. Are you not of more value than they? Which of you by worrying can add one cubit to his stature?

In other words, stop worrying. We are reminded to not worry about the needs that God promises to supply. Some of the ill effects of worrying are stress and damage to our health, disruption in our productivity, the positive treatment of others will start to wane, and we become consumed with the worrisome thoughts. Of course there is a reduction of the trust that God will see us through. We will be cared for. He is looking out for us. Our focus must shift from allowing people and things to define us to seeking out the perfect will of the Father, who knows the beginning from the end. He has so marvelously carved out a niche and a righteous pathway for us and specifically for those who will obey and trust in his word.

Further in the chapter, verse thirty-three states, "But seek first the kingdom of God and His righteousness, and all these things shall be added to you," which means to turn to God first for help in any endeavor, take His character as our pattern, and serve and obey Him in everything. Material things, people, and goals all compete to become a priority in our life. What is it that is really important? Any of those things mentioned can cause us to displace God in our life if we do not actively with enthusiasm choose to give Him first place in our life in every area.

Faith and trust. Trust and faith. For it is declared in Psalm 119:105, "Your word *is* a lamp to my feet, and a light to my path." Therefore, it is walking in the illumination of His word that provides us the supplementation of God's purpose in our lives. Our ability to trust Him and patiently wait on Him strengthens our resolve and fortifies our spirit, believing that whatever God promises has to come to pass.

We must know within our heart of hearts that God never makes empty promises and that what God has spoken and declared must come to pass. For in Isaiah 55:11, His word declares, "So shall my word be that goes forth out of my mouth, it shall not return to me void, but it shall accomplish that which I please and it shall prosper in the thing for which I sent it." Understand that His word is much greater than our thinking or planning. We would be foolish to try to fit God into our mold and make His plans and purposes conform to our ways. On the contrary, we must strive to fit into *His* plans. The results are much more rewarding.

In taking this journey, our faith and hope must rest in knowing and trusting *Him,* that *He* will secure our future through His word, knowing that what *He* says has to come to pass—in His appointed time. Along the way we have to be mindful of our responsibility in our own journey. Even though the map has been charted, it is up to us to be morally responsible for the choices, tasks, and decisions that we make in our existence. We must not allow the opinions of others to define who we are or hinder our journey to live out our purpose in life. For if we depend on the voices of people to orchestrate our lives, we will never catch on to the rhythm of life. We have to grab hold of our destiny and never settle for less as we strive for a productive life. This role has been written for us. No substitute will do.

We can learn a lesson in this from Jesus when He was at the wedding in Cana. His mother knew that He was special and a fulfillment of a promise from God. When she felt she saw an opportunity for Jesus to reveal Himself to the world, she tried to get Him to perform, on her terms, a miracle. However Jesus, being in tune with the Holy Spirit, knew that it was not His time. We are reminded of the words that he spoke in John 2:4: "Jesus said to her, 'Woman, what does your concern have to do with Me? My hour has not yet come.'" He was willing to wait on God, instead of being influenced by his mother. Can God trust us to wait on Him, in spite of the masses of people that will come into our life that will try to get us to operate out of our season?

Jesus' ability to tune out the flesh and listen to the spirit enabled Him to perform His first miracle in the Bible by having the patience to allow God to orchestrate His path. The Bible teaches us in Proverbs 3:5–6, "Trust in the Lord with all your heart, and lean not on your own understanding. In all your ways acknowledge Him, and he shall direct your paths." It is God who wants to direct our paths, for He has a clear path for our lives, and when we allow people and things to clutter our vision and ability to hear, we stand the chance to forfeit the true will of God for our lives. We must trust in the path that has been established for us upon the foundation of the world.

He knows the direction that He is leading us in, and even though we may face challenges and obstacles, we must take solace in knowing that whatever route He has taken us to or is taking us to, in the end it will work out for the good. The Bible teaches us in Psalm 37:23, "The steps of a *good* man are ordered by the Lord, and He delights in his way." In other words, the person in whom God delights is the one who trusts and follows God, and tries to do His will. God will watch over this person and make firm every step they take. We should seek His advice before we step out if we would like God to direct our way. He has stated many times that He is there for us. Trust and believe.

The message here is that life is a process, and every step has a lesson to teach us. Nobody really buys a house for its steps, and yet oftentimes the steps are vitally important. Sometimes they allow us to gain access to certain properties to gain connection to an entrance. If the property has an upstairs then they become a means to reaching our destiny, which may lie at a higher level. Just as they are used to access various areas in a house or other buildings, they're also used to ascend to certain purposes in our life. We must be careful how we approach steps, for a misstep can cause delays, injuries, and, in some cases, death. God uses this process to prepare us in reaching our destiny. For some it is a long and tedious journey, while for others it can be quick and exuberant. We do not determine the path; He does. We only control how we choose to travel down the path that has been designed for us.

We should not allow people to determine who we are, and most certainly should not give anyone authorization to question our self-worth. Stay committed and grant God's perfect will to be the compass for our journey. The ultimate GPS, *He* knows which way is best for us.

First Corinthians 15:58 states, "Therefore, my beloved brethren, be steadfast, immovable, always abounding in the work of the Lord, knowing that your labor is not in vain in the Lord," which means that nothing we do is in vain because of the resurrection. There are times that we neglect to do the right thing because we fail to see the results. However, if we can continue to cultivate that heavenly perspective, we will soon understand that often we won't see the good results from our efforts. Therefore, truly believing that Christ won the ultimate victory must have a direct effect on the way we live right now.

Again, we should not allow the opinion of people to define us or hinder our purpose in life. For if we depend on the voices of other people to orchestrate our lives, we will never catch on to the rhythm of life and live a productive life. We have to grab hold of our destiny, never settling for less. This role has been written for us, and no substitute will do.

QUESTIONS FOR "THE PATH":

1] What steps have you taken to prepare yourself for the path that God has chosen for you?

a] _____
_____
_____
_____
_____

2] What has God spoken to you concerning your destiny?

a] _____
_____
_____
_____
_____

(2)
STAY FOCUSED

Faith in God is I believe therefore I see, not the other way around—seeing before believing. For we walk by faith and not by sight. Keeping our focus on what is eternal, and not on temporary things. This should be the stronghold of our faith. The belief in things hoped for, that our five senses cannot corrupt.

Having faith in our vision is very much a big part of succeeding, and preparing ourselves is another part. "Chance favors only the prepared mind," according to Louis Pasteur. As we deal with the ebb and flow of life along with the hustle and bustle of our personal life, we must remain attentive and conscientious of our main purpose in this thing called life. What is that? What is our "main" purpose? It is to be productive for the Kingdom of God at all times.

Prioritizing our life in such a fashion that would allow us to live in a positive, productive, and progressive manner is imperative and requires faith in the way of the Word. We must never allow the cares of the world to overtake our view of that assignment, or get sidetracked of that purpose that has been created for us. Proverbs 4:25 states, "Let your eyes look straight ahead and your eyelids look right before you."

Setting goals for ourselves will serve as a compass for success. It creates a discipline and direction in order for acquisition to be had; sort of like staying in your lane so that you can obtain what you set out for. There may be times that the road gets bumpy and pothole-filled, accompanied by an array of obstacles, and then frustration somehow sneaks its way into our psyche. Leon Trotsky said, "Life is not an easy matter . . . You cannot live through it without falling into frustration and cynicism unless you have before you a great idea which raises you above personal misery, above weakness, above all kinds of perfidy and baseness."

Is life unfair? At times, yes. Do we sometimes have unrealistic expectations? Of course we do. We all have a tendency to *plan* to overachieve—meaning that we sometimes set unreal expectations of ourselves. It's like the baseball player who wants to get a home run every time he comes up to bat. Because his plan has no balances, he fails miserably; it's all or nothing with him. Instead of using wisdom and appreciating the objective, which is to get on base, his unrealistic goals put him in a position of pure embarrassment from which he could not bounce back. Instead of changing his attitude (which in turn would affect his mindset), which would translate into better decision making (thus producing better results), he chose to remain arrogant, blaming everyone else for his shortcomings and didn't realize just how close he was to fulfilling his destiny. I know that life may appear impossible at times. The closer we get to happiness, the more obstacles get in the way. The problem is not life, but how we view it. Stop expecting life to get easier and learn to embrace the challenges. Everyone feels the same pain, just in different ways. When life feels too painful, allow God to be your Motrin.

Perhaps we should use Jesus as a model for perseverance. No matter what was going on around Him, He kept His focus on the task at hand. Even if they were saying "Hosanna" or "Crucify him," He stayed on point, focused and prepared. He understood His mission, which was to do the will of His Father. Whether He was at a wedding or a funeral, He stayed true to His purpose. His assignment was clear, and He never wavered. As believers, we must stay focused in an ever-changing environment.

Humility is an acquired taste that has to be appreciated when traveling that road to meeting goals. Many of us that set goals find that the trek will present situations that will have us questioning our moral compasses, our sanity, our patience, and even the desire to continue on. Philippians 2:5–8 teaches us about the humbled and exalted Christ. It states:

> Let this mind be in you which was also in Christ Jesus, who, being in the form of God, did not consider it robbery to be equal with God, but made Himself of no reputation, taking the form of a bondservant, *and* coming in the likeness of men. And being found in appearance as a man, He humbled Himself and became obedient to *the point of* death, even the death of the cross.

For the road on which God takes us may not be glamorous or friendly, but we must take comfort in knowing that He will not put more on us than we can bear. Understanding that will also enable us to stay focused on the task at hand and maintain our composure at all times. Proper choices based upon our options will always keep us on the road to our goals. Jesus, when being tempted by the enemy in the wilderness after the forty-day fast, defeated Satan with the Word, for every temptation the enemy brought His way, Jesus responded with the word. He stayed cool, calm, and collected. He stayed focused. He understood that the word would withstand any attack against Him. We as believers have the same promise and weapon at our disposal, if we would just utilize it. The key is to believe God when He said He would never leave us nor forsake us.

God's word teaches us in Psalm 91:5–6, "You shall not be afraid of the terror by night, *Nor* of the arrow that flies by day, *Nor* of the pestilence that walks in darkness, *Nor* of the destruction that lays waste at noonday." Does life seem unfair? Seemingly, yes. Does it appear that our expectations are unrealistic? I know it can be impossible at times. The closer you get to happiness, the more obstacles get in the way. The problem is not life but how you view it. Stop expecting life to get easier and learn to embrace the challenges. Everyone feels the same pain, just in different ways. When life feels like it's too painful, allow God to be your aspirin, your sedative, and your ibuprofen. Without setting goals, we haphazardly stumble about. Then frustration sets in.

The enemy knows how valuable we are to the kingdom, so he does everything in his power to keep us from reaching our destination. That's why we must allow our Lord Jesus Christ to be our example and model for staying focused and not permitting the difficult situations around us to cancel out the promises that He has declared for our lives. Thus, as believers we must be diligent in all of our efforts to please the master, trusting Him at His word, and by obeying, which guarantees us success in the endeavors that have been promised by the Father, through His holy word.

Although we start out with good intentions, there will be times when our faith will falter. This doesn't automatically mean we have failed. As we learn in Matthew 14:22–31 redemption is ours:

Immediately Jesus made His disciples get into the boat and go before Him to the other side, while He sent the multitudes away. And when He had sent the multitudes away, He went up on the mountain by Himself to pray. Now when evening came, He was alone there. But the boat was now in the middle of the sea, tossed by the waves, for the wind was contrary. Now in the fourth watch of the night Jesus went to them, walking on the sea. And when the disciples saw Him walking on the sea, they were troubled, saying, "It is a ghost!" And they cried out for fear. But immediately Jesus spoke to them, saying, "Be of good cheer! It is I; do not be afraid." And Peter answered Him and said, "Lord, if it is You, command me to come to You on the water." So He said, "Come." And when Peter had come down out of the boat, he walked on the water to go to Jesus. But when he saw that the wind *was* boisterous, he was afraid; and beginning to sink he cried out, saying, "Lord, save me!" And immediately Jesus stretched out *His* hand and caught him, and said to him, "O you of little faith, why did you doubt?"

You see, many of us are like Peter. We start out fine and steady but then permit the cares of the world to cause us to sink before reaching our destiny. We must remain levelheaded and focus on the task at hand, at the same time understanding that storms will rise up in our lives that will try to deter us from reaching our goals, our purpose. We must learn from Peter, who started out focusing on the answer but then began sinking when he allowed the moment to be greater than the answer before him, which was Jesus. Regardless of the circumstances and how we feel, or whatever the storm is that is raging in our life, we must reach out and wrap our faith around God's unchanging character. We must constantly remind ourselves when we are weary and frustrated that we have a Heavenly Father who will never leave us or forsake us.

The realization that there will be situations that will come along and stretch our faith must be a part of our consciousness. Most times in the beginning of the storm, God is not readily visible to us, sometimes things have to get worse before they start to get better. However, we must hold on strong to our faith, knowing in the end that it will work out for the good. When we feel abandoned, we must dig in deep and find praise in spite of our feelings and press our way into worship. For we must be committed to the things of God, not offering Him our spare time or spare change; we must be willing to give Him our all. That means surrendering all of our heart, soul, mind, body, and strength to Him.

Staying focused on the conditions of God requires discipline; we must intentionally come before His presence with praise and thanksgiving, honoring Him with the fruits from our lips to the pleasing of His ear. When we are faced with spiritual dryness, we must allow the moisture of God's promises to enrich us and sustain us with the comprehension that in this walk with the Lord there will be moments when we will go through a dry season — a wilderness experience — where it seems desolate and spiritually dry, when no fruit appears in our life; the harder we try to make something happen, the more frustrated we become.

I believe that it is at these times that we have to reflect back and appreciate all the great and wonderful things that God has provided us with thus far. This should and will motivate us to seek after the Lord and reinvest in our prayers like never before and then gravitate to His word seeking His wisdom and direction; holding on to His unchanged hands. Growth is often painful and scary. Change is inevitable; therefore we must be willing to let go of our old ways to experience the new things. Embracing this kind of mindset will cause us to be misunderstood and often ostracized by people who want us to major on the minor.

As saints of God who have an assignment to complete, we cannot be delayed by worrying about things that we cannot change. Colossians 3:1–2 states, "If ye then be risen with Christ, seek those things which are above, where Christ sitteth on the right hand of God. Set your affection on things above, not on things on the earth." The Bible teaches us to focus on things that are above and not on the minor, temporary inconveniences. We must entertain a new perspective on things, if you will. We change our moral and ethical behaviors by letting Christ live within us, so that we can be shaped into what we should be. We become mission bound with purpose and a calling to achieve. Therefore, it is imperative that we not lose our focus.

As a result we must then organize our life in such a way that we become more effective. Many people fail to organize themselves, and for that reason they fail to maximize the opportunities that are given to them, consequently settling for less and then getting mired in frustration. Disorganized people generally permit themselves to respond to the emotional needs rather than proceeding in a logical path with regard to the things that are going on around them. They fail to grasp the importance of managing themselves better to be more effective. By organizing our mindset, we have a corrective to apply when things seemingly appear to be going wrong, thus realizing that there is nothing ignominious about admitting an error. In fact, once humility is owned, we find ourselves in the minority of recognizing that we don't have to be perfect. Just be willing to be used by God.

We must also learn patience when things don't go our way and as planned with the understanding that God is not working on our time but vice versa. Patience is one of the fruits of the Holy Spirit. It's a word derived from the Latin word that means, "to suffer." Sometimes we will be challenged to wait patiently, even to endure some tribulations without complaint. There will be some times that we must exhibit a propensity to bear pain or handle trouble without losing self-control or becoming a disturbance to others. How you handle a situation speaks volumes to those that bear witness, near and far.

We are reminded in James of the patience we are to demonstrate when we find ourselves in turmoil. James 1:2–4 states, "My brethren, count it all joy when you fall into various trials, knowing that the testing of your faith produces patience. But let patience have *its* perfect work, that you may be perfect and complete, lacking nothing." James doesn't say *if* you face trials, but *when* you face trials. It is assumed that we will have trials and that it is possible to profit from them. The bottom line is not to pretend to be happy when we face adversity, but to have a positive outlook because of what trials can produce in our lives. The mature believer must realize that God will use delayed gratification to accomplish His perfect work inside our lives.

Hence, as we face problems and circumstances, we develop a deeper appreciation of God, which causes us to rely on His word that much more. Some of the greatest worship you will ever experience with God will come through your brokenness and pain. When you feel abandoned by Him, it will trigger some of your most authentic prayers and produce some of your most thunderous shouts. As you stay anchored in the awesome promises of Him, He will continue to guide you through every storm you face.

Matthew 7:24–27 asserts,

> Therefore whoever hears these sayings of Mine, and does them, I will liken him to a wise man who built his house on the rock: and the rain descended, the floods came, and the winds blew and beat on that house; and it did not fall, for it was founded on the rock. But everyone who hears these sayings of Mine, and does not do them, will be like a foolish man who built his house on the sand: and the rain descended, the floods came, and the winds blew and beat on that house; and it fell. And great was its fall.

Remember, whatever you build will be tried by numerous elements, and only what you do for the Lord will stand. So stay focused and keep God in the forefront.

QUESTION FOR "STAY FOCUSED":

1] List three (3) ways to keep you focused on what God has spokenconcerning your destiny.

a] _____
_____
_____
_____

2] Do you spend any amount of time meditating on your destiny?If so, how much?

a] _____
_____
_____
_____

3] What causes you not to be focused on your destiny?

a] _____
_____
_____
_____

(3)

Activating Your Faith

Faith

*Into one's life, it will
cloud your consciousness.
Bouts of depression
have been championed.
Carried like a backpack
you can right a wrong.
Understanding the need
while hugging the floor
with your knees
will enable you to heed
the powers that it breeds
putting growth to seeds.
Having just a bit of this, and
perseverance
becomes a friend.
"It" manifest trust in
the oddest of situations.
"Keep the ¼." is a
mainstay in our vocation.
Knowing in time "it"
can and will provide hope.
With "it" in mind
Struggles, difficulties¼
you're fitted to cope.*

Do you know what I'm
talking about?
This thing you should keep
that allows you to anticipate
waking up from your sleep.

Talking 'bout faith. Something you should have
for without it, ya' know your soul is your bail.

In order to reach the destination that God has created in our life, we must develop great faith in His word for our life. Faith is essential to having any success in our God-given vision and assignment. For any task, personal or otherwise, to be accomplished, we must have faith that it will get done. Believing Him at his word is vital to success.

Hebrews 11:1 teaches us that " . . . faith is the substance of things hope for and the evidence of things not seen." We have to be conscientious of the fact that if God has said a thing or a concept, it will come to pass. We must walk in confidence in His word, as well as in our ability to carry out the assignment, which He places in our spirit. Knowing that in the due season, our season, it will speak and not lie, for if He says it, that thing, just as He has promised, will come to pass.

This vision isn't some mystical quality or gift that comes out of a vacuum, or something that can be found indiscriminately in some second-hand store, as some people believe. As adults, we sometimes forget that there are things bigger than us and our simplistic endeavors. Understanding the faith that was taught to us as children will prepare us for any questionable life task. Praying for a better understanding should be a preeminent application in our daily routine. It must be birthed out of that piece of our being that has been stirred in our heart, from a desire within, from the depths of who we are and what we are to believe.

Faith must be that vehicle that drives us to the place of completion. It must also incorporate the help of those whom it was meant to attract. It must be like a magnet that unites, solicits, and challenges people, especially those along our trek to understanding our purpose. For true visionaries have the ability to be great listeners and discerners, to weed out and grasp what is needful to them and to God, as well as paying attention to that which is hurtful, with an eye out for the enemy.

No one person can accomplish every great thing alone. To fulfill things that will have an everlasting impact on people's lives, we will need adequate help. Additionally, to be successful, it would be wise to identify someone who has mastered that which we are trying to accomplish, someone who would give sound advice and can help to sharpen our skills.

God must be at the forefront and the conclusion in order for us to have any measure of success. In Him are the tools that are greater than our limited capabilities. We must believe! Knowing that success must be navigated through the uncompromising word of the Lord will reap huge rewards. For Proverbs 29:18 states, "Where there is no revelation, the people cast off restraint; but happy is he who keeps the law." In other words, a prophetic vision will shed light on the task at hand, as long as God's ways are adhered too.

A true vision, shrouded in faith, then becomes indispensable for a genuine visionary. It's the fuel that ignites his vehicle to reveal his passion and reach his destiny. No great or elaborate work orchestrated by God, who should always remain in the forefront, will ever come back void. It will rally finances and any other resources needed to complete its mission. The greater the vision, the more potential it will provide for participation, as well as recipients.

Reminding us that the just should live by faith, Habakkuk 2:2–3 reads, "Then the LORD answered me and said: 'Write the vision and make *it* plain on tablets, that he may run who reads it. For the vision *is* yet for an appointed time, but at the end it will speak, and it will not lie. Though it tarries, wait for it; because it will surely come, it will not tarry.'" We will learn that God's words to Habakkuk would be the same words that He would say to us: "Be patient! I will work out my plans for you in my perfect timing." We must then be patient and understand that everything has a season and reasoning about it.

Consequently, we must remain confident with our vision and steadfast in our faith. For Hebrews 11:6 says, "But without faith *it is* impossible to please *Him,* for he who comes to God must believe that He is, and *that* He is a rewarder of those who diligently seek Him." Oftentimes, we make the mistake of assuming that we must bring the vision to pass, leaning on our own limited ideas. True faith comes from hearing a word from God and trusting the instructions that have been given and then watching God make the provision to bring it to pass.

Abraham was told by God "to get thee out" of his country and from around his kindred. He was not told where his final destination would be, but just to trust God at his word. Just imagine that for a minute. Imagine if the Almighty would ask you to give up everything and trust him. Could you walk in obedience, or would the things that you have grown accustomed to hinder you from moving forward? We as believers must be like our father of faith, Abraham, willing to trust God when he could not envision or understand God's reasoning behind it.

Real anointed and successful people aren't successful because they always get it right; they achieve great things because they have the propensity and the resilience to pick themselves up and try again in the midst of failure. May I offer to you that it's through our failures and our struggles that we get a real sense of how strong our faith truly is. It's when giving up would be so easy and safe, but enduring another round would be so much more rewarding when we pull up our bootstraps and say, "Even though I can't trace you, I am still going to trust you."

We will become endowed with fresh energy that will propel us to go further in the things that are purposed in our life. The three Hebrew boys surely must have felt that way when Nebuchadnezzar gave them an option to either abide by the decree he set over the province or be cast into the furnace. Not just any furnace, but a burning, fiery furnace. It would have been so easy to agree to the edict set forth by the king; however, their love and faith gave them boldness that they would trust God and His plan for their lives rather than lean on their own understanding. How many of us miss the true purpose of our lives by caving in to the pressure?

We must realize that the plans God has for our lives are greater than the obstacles we face, and if we would activate our faith, we could live a much more productive life, than simply settling and living a mediocre and uninspiring life. So, believe the scripture, notably where the word of the Lord declares to us in Proverbs 3: 5–6, "Trust in the Lord with all your heart, and lean not on your own understanding; in all your ways acknowledge him, and He shall direct your paths."

In order to fulfill our destiny, we must allow God's perfect will for our lives to manifest by our ability to trust him at his word. Remember there is a wealth of talent and potential buried inside of us just waiting for the opportunity to be released and to guide us to a place of fulfillment. There's an old Japanese proverb: "Some people let one-time failures thwart their dreams, but successful people use failure as stepping stones toward their next level of success; fall seven times and stand up eight." Therefore, let faith be the springboard we use to propel us toward the things that have been prepared for us. Destiny awaits us. Don't be caught sleeping during the time we should be excelling.

Another perfect example of activating our faith is the scenario the Prophet Elijah found himself faced with. He was living through a season of drought, where the land had dried, and the cattle and all other livestock had died out. He received a word from the Lord that an abundance of rain was coming. Imagine living in a drought, where you have lost everything, both finances and peace of mind. The conditions that at one point seemed so secure were now all of a sudden out of his control. Well, that's what the man of God faced: dire straits.

However, he exhibited the way to come out of this distressful situation. He held steadfastly onto the promise and the word of the Lord. When we are faced with trials and tribulations, when the road is filled with turmoil, we have to be resilient, with that fervor within our character that causes us to rely on our faith for support and results. We repeatedly make the mistake of trying to figure it out, instead of trusting in His word and allowing it to accordingly work itself out.

Elijah, the prophet, heard the sound of abundance but saw despair. He got into the birthing position and began to pray what he believed was in his spirit to come out, but there was nothing manifesting. He sent his servant seven times waiting for the manifestation to come. Faith had to be exhibited over and over. This is not for the impatient person that wants instantaneous results. No, it's for that confident person who has the propensity to wait on the Lord throughout the vicissitudes of the event. It's for those that will anchor their belief on what was spoken and then allow it to manifest.

Activating our faith is essential to obtain the things that God has for us. For His words declare unto us without faith it is impossible to please Him. So, to receive all of the promises and provisions that have been allocated to us, our faith must be activated. When it's registered in Heaven, we will experience an enriched life, full of the promise that has been designed for us by the Father.

When Elijah finally received the promise from God, it came in the form of a fist, much like the size of a human hand. Nevertheless, out of this small image was the abundance that had been bottled up for three-and-a-half years. Can we trust and believe God when what He gives us does not look like what we had envisioned in our spirit and mind? Elijah labored and toiled, and when his servant finally noticed something, it did not look like much at first.

Too often we miss opportunities in life because what we see doesn't look like much, and it is at these times that we fail to understand the concept of seedtime and harvest. Are we forfeiting a blessing because our perception is not allowing us to grab ahold of what God has in store for us? His word teaches us to not have disdain for the small beginnings. When Elijah, who was working hard when he heard of the sign, began to activate his faith by running to tell King Ahab what was happening, he was so overcome by the joy of this great manifestation that he outran chariots.

We must understand that whenever something resonates in our spirit, it will give us awesome power. A supernatural feeling will enable us to overcome all obstacles and to do things that others won't understand and can't perform themselves. Our promised land and destiny is waiting on us to activate our faith and walk into all God has for us. So activate your faith now and enjoy His riches and glory.

QUESTIONS FOR "ACTIVATING YOUR FAITH":

1] How do you build your faith on a daily basis?

a] _____
_____
_____
_____

2] How does your faith or lack of faith affect your destiny?

a] _____
_____
_____
_____

3] List four (4) characteristics of faith.

a] _____
_____
_____
_____

(4)
JUST DO YOU

Ever since the day you came into this world
nothing seems to satisfy you.
All you do is complain.
So do you believe, you never catch a break
and everybody else get the sunshine
and all you get is pouring rain?

Well, if you don't like the way you've been born, try being born again.

Too often in life, we spend countless hours in stagnation, looking at others fulfilling their destiny. Because of some of our hang-ups and insecurities, we begin to feel inferior. Foolishly, we assume that we are the only flawed person in the world and that the persons that are reaching their destination are flawless. It is this mindset that keeps us from being progressive and living a rich and rewarding life.

As mentioned before, the way we view life could be a hindrance. Have you ever once considered that the only thing that's holding us back from soaring like an eagle is the way we see yourself? We must learn how to appreciate ourselves and then change our attitudes and behaviors to get out of the rut in which we repeatedly find ourselves. Being overly critical of our own faults, our weaknesses, and our missteps can lead to low spirits and a sense of hopelessness. We then dig a psychological hole that takes a herculean effort of which to climb out.

There are areas in all our lives that need improvement. We *all* have these areas, and each day we awake, we must strive to correct, revamp, and upgrade our situations to understand the new opportunities that are presented to obtain better results and positive change. One of the worst things we can do is to go through life being against oneself. Although, this battle against oneself can be won, we must avoid comparing ourselves to other people.

No two people are alike. We may have kinship and comparisons, but we are uniquely different in how we handle things and the way we observe life. In a recent study done by European psychiatrist Alfred Adler, he found that ninety-five percent of the population tends to compare themselves unfavorably to others. It is comparisons like this that causes individuals to live in misery and inadequacy.

This is why we must strive to *enjoy* life and identify the positive things about ourselves instead of always focusing on the negative components. Our Lord and Savior, Jesus, taught us to love our neighbors as we love ourselves; however take notice that He purposely shows us that our love for others should be no greater than the love for oneself. This is why it is important to feel good about ourselves and not be so unforgiving of our own shortcomings. Remember that you cannot truly love someone if you don't truly love yourself.

It is the enemy's task to try and distort your mind and create distractions that will keep us from moving in our promise. Notice how God's servant, Moses, at times felt inadequate when God wanted to bring the children of Israel out of bondage. According to Exodus 3:11–12:

> But Moses said to God, "Who *am* I that I should go to Pharaoh, and that I should bring the children of Israel out of Egypt?" So He said, "I will certainly be with you. And this *shall be* a sign to you that I have sent you: When you have brought the people out of Egypt, you shall serve God on this mountain."

God Himself assured Moses that He would be with him every step of the journey, and yet, Moses still could not get past his fears and insecurities. His previous perspective almost caused him to miss his appointed time of greatness. As believers, we must possess the aptitude that would allow us to be intelligent enough to look past our failures and weaknesses to realize that we are a work in progress, remembering to thank God along the way, each and every day for the progress that we see.

This vision comes with understanding that the word of the Lord declares in Psalm 37:23: "The steps of a *good* man are ordered by the Lord, and He delights in his way," which means that the individual God captivates is one that follows God, trusts, and has faith in Him, and tries to do His will. God guards, protects, and makes firm every step that individual takes.

Our movements are orchestrated and carefully considered. We are methodically given assignments to carry out. We are supplied with everything we need to complete our assignments; the only requirement is to follow the instructions that are given by God, trusting completely even when it doesn't make sense to the flesh. We are commanded to listen, hearken diligently, and carry out the mandate. Then, we are guaranteed to succeed.

Moses almost forfeited his destiny focusing on his hang-ups, his problem areas. In Exodus 4:10–12, God explains his position in Moses life, our life, when Moses latched onto his shortcomings.

> Then Moses said to the LORD, "O my Lord, I *am* not eloquent, neither before nor since You have spoken to Your servant; but I *am* slow of speech and slow of tongue. So the LORD said to him, "Who has made man's mouth? Or who makes the mute, the deaf, the seeing, or the blind? *Have* not I, the LORD? Now therefore, go, and I will be with your mouth and teach you what you shall say."

You see, each of us every day generally has internal dialogues and inner conversations with ourselves throughout the day. The problem is most times, if we are not careful, we will allow negative thoughts to permeate our minds. Moses' slow speech was an attempt to deflect from God's purpose in his life. Moses interpreted God's will as a hurdle, when in reality Moses dwelled on his own shortcomings, causing him to almost walk away from his destiny, just like the enemy does with us — using tactics to get us to walk away and turn our backs on what is rightfully ours.

However, I've got great news. In spite of the obstacles in everybody's way to greatness, all we have to do is be patient, faithful, and calm; then it will be revealed that we are the right person for the chosen assignment. Hurdles only build character and strength. We should just stay focused and believe in ourselves. Let opposition motivate us, instead of permitting it to destroy us. We should be happy in who we are, enjoy ourselves, and know that our season is right around the corner. Remember God uses the foolish things to confound the wise.

Here's some more good news: God's power shows up strongest in our weakest points, for when we are weak, He is strong. So, instead of continually criticizing and being stuck in that negative mode, take some time and enjoy ourselves and our life. Start believing in the fact that we are unique and one of a kind and stop auditioning to play the part of someone else when the role He is giving us is for a lifetime. Always remember that creativity and uniqueness lie inside of us, just waiting to come out and flourish. All that has to happen is for us to release that blessing and let it do what it was designed to do.

Second Corinthians 5:17 states, "Therefore, if anyone *is* in Christ, *he is* a new creation; old things have passed away; behold, all things have become new." Newness! Newness! That's what happens when we envelop His word and discover our course. So, when opposition and hurdles try to rise up against us, the word is on our side declaring, "I am a new creation." It is imperative that to remind ourselves on a daily basis that our yesterday is behind us. Trust and believe that if God did not have anything more for us, He wouldn't have awakened us today. That fact in and of itself is an indication that there's more for us to do.

Keep in mind that we are relevant, so stay focused and just do you.

QUESTIONS FOR "JUST DO YOU":

1] Briefly describe who you are or who you see yourself to be.

a] _____
_____
_____
_____

2] What steps have you taken to prepare yourself to fulfill what God has spoken concerning you?

a] _____
_____
_____
_____

3] Are you willing to make the necessary changes needed to fulfill your destiny? Explain.

a] _____
_____
_____
_____

(5)

Understanding the Transitional stage

My family, frankly, they weren't folks who went to church every week. My mother was one of the most spiritual people I knew, but she didn't raise me in the church, so I came to my Christian faith later in life, and it was because the precepts of Jesus Christ spoke to me in terms of the kind of life that I would want to lead. *-Barack Obama*

Every so often in life, we are face with a transitional stage, a fork in the road, if you will. It is at this stage that the challenges of life are on full display. The choices and decisions that are made at this stage can be beneficial or detrimental to the task at hand; an awkward stage to say the least. As a believer, it is at this time where faith, trust, endurance, patience, and perseverance are tested the most. The Bible teaches us to let patience have its perfect work.

We see in the case of Israel, when God was bringing the Israelites out of bondage to the "Land of Promise," which flowed with milk, honey, and fruits. Now, even though their bodies had escaped Egypt, their minds were still stuck in bondage. It was in this transitional period that highlights how holding onto the past and not letting go can lead to unfavorable results. There, in the midst of this tremendous undertaking, as God was delivering the people of Israel out of bondage, we saw people that held onto the past, who refuse to let go, that eventually died in the wilderness—all because they refused to control their anxieties and understand that God was providing a way. They could not submit, or refused to accede, to the will of God.

The miracle that would deliver and liberate them from the bondage that they had endured for quite some time was of no relevance. Their problem was that they had become so used to the familiar, and were afraid of the unknown, which prevented them from reaching their destination. The realization is that all too often we allow the fear of what's ahead of us from fulfilling the assignments and ascending to the destination that God has prepared for us.

In Israel's case, thousands of people that crossed over the Red Sea had to die because they could not let go of the past. In a parallel sense, even in our lives, there are things, situations, and conditions that have to die in order for us to reach our destiny. Consequently, in some cases, toxic relationships that are not beneficial for our well-being have to die out in the transitional period. In other cases, there's a troubling family member who's a hindrance to our progression to destiny that has to be disconnected from us, so that subsequently we won't have to carry that excessive baggage along for our journey in our transition.

It is along this stage that trust is well tested and tried; it is the place where you cannot be moved by circumstances or people, but by your allegiance to God and Him alone. This is the period where the enemy tempts us to forfeit our promise and stay in bondage, up under his control. We are taught in Hebrews 10: 35–38:

> Therefore do not cast away your confidence, which has great reward. For you have need of endurance, so that after you have done the will of God, you may receive the promise. For yet a little while, *And* He who is coming will come and

will not tarry. Now the just shall live by faith; but if anyone draws back, my soul has no pleasure in him.

We are encouraged in our belief as Christians to persevere in our faith and conduct when we're facing any type of affliction and pressure. Character building and patience are usually the results of suffering. Although we won't admit it, it's good for us. It's during these times of great stress that we should find clarity or feel God's presence more clearly and find help from other believers that we thought never cared. Having faith and trust that He is with us in our times of need ensures that we will be successful in our endeavors.

There's always an avenue where the enemy will try to tangle up something in us to hold us back; if you are physically healthy, then he will try to affect your mental stability. In view of the fact that the enemy knows humans are triune. The only way to be completely whole is to be one in body, soul, and spirit, but he will try his hardest to keep one of these aspects entangled in confusion so that he can have a foothold and keep us from reaching our destiny, and fulfilling our God-given promises.

The process of transition can bring about many challenges, which will often stretch our faith and cause us to find that inner strength. We often find ourselves having to go through a waiting period that will seem as if time has stood still, whereas believers feel as though the promises of God are never coming to pass. It is in this season that our patience is being tried and tested, giving us that opportunity to grow in our faith and to widen our trust and confidence in God. In this waiting period our motives and attitudes are purified, allowing us to come face to face with our own impure, selfish, and proud motives that can easily cloud and hinder our judgment. This is where the enemy turns up the heat and sends spirits of aggravation and frustration in an attempt to abort our journey to the place that God has created for us.

We learn about opposing forces in Exodus 17:8–14:

> Now Amalek came and fought with Israel in Rephidim. And Moses said to Joshua, "Choose us some men and go out, fight with Amalek. Tomorrow I will stand on the top of the hill with the rod of God in my hand." So Joshua did as Moses said to him, and fought with Amalek. And Moses, Aaron, and Hur went up to the top of the hill. And so it was, when Moses held up his hand, that Israel prevailed; and when he let down his hand, Amalek prevailed. But Moses' hands *became* heavy; so they took a stone and put *it* under him, and he sat on it. And Aaron and Hur supported his hands, one on one side, and the other on the other side; and his hands were steady until the going down of the sun. So Joshua defeated Amalek and his people with the edge of the sword." Then the LORD said to Moses, "Write this *for* a memorial in the book and recount *it* in the hearing of Joshua, that I will utterly blot out the remembrance of Amalek from under heaven."

Have we identified the Amalek in our life, that element that fights us in transition? For Israel the Amalekites stood in opposition, trying to prevent them from reaching the Promised Land. What's keeping us from reaching our appointed place? Do we know that our God has equipped us with everything we need to succeed? Whether it's a difficult marriage, a trying job, or a troubled child, we can do all things through Christ that strengthens us. So, we must press our way through opposing forces while keeping our focus on the promise of God, all the while understanding that this too shall pass.

Too often we get caught up in a cycle of mishaps because we fail to create an environment that is conducive to where we are headed; instead we get bogged down on the failures of our past. We never take the time to surround ourselves with the trendsetters and the pioneers who can bring a wealth of experience, expertise, and stature to our lives. We would rather limit our circle and then complain about the time frame and the place in which we find ourselves. I suggest that there are many navigational systems in life. The mentors, pastors, teachers, parents, and prayer which can direct you to that place that will be productive for you.

So in your time of transition soak up as much knowledge as possible, embrace change, and be willing to adapt, knowing you are not alone. Even when you don't get the response you were looking for, just know that God is on the throne. Trust that God will bring us healing when we are hurt, peace when we are troubled, and strength when we are weak just as He did for Daniel in the passage of Daniel 10:12–14 where it points out,

> Then he said to me, "Do not fear, Daniel, for from the first day that you set your heart to understand, and to humble yourself before your God, your words were heard; and I have come because of your words. But the prince of the kingdom of Persia withstood me twenty-one days; and behold, Michael, one of the chief princes, came to help me, for I had been left alone there with the kings of Persia. Now I have come to make you understand what will happen to your people in the latter days, for the vision *refers* to *many* days yet *to come.*"

Like Daniel in this transitional period, many of us may face and encounter spiritual opposition to the assignment we have been given. The warfare we face causes us to grow stronger in the spirit. It serves as dumbbells in that the more we overcome them, the stronger we become. Realizing that, we are reminded in 2 Corinthians,

> For the weapons of our warfare *are* not carnal but mighty in God for pulling down strongholds, casting down arguments and every high thing that exalts itself against the knowledge of God, bringing every thought into captivity to the obedience of Christ.

So, relax and stay cool, calm, and collected knowing that if we walk in the will of the Lord, He will protect us and guide us in this time of transition.

QUESTIONS FOR
"UNDERSTANDING THE TRANSITIONAL STAGE":

1] Do you believe that you are in a season of transition? If yes, explain.

a] _____
_____
_____
_____

2] During your transitional stage, what has God shown you concerning your strengths and weaknesses?

a] _____
_____
_____
_____

(6)
SUBMISSION

> The reason why many are still troubled, still seeking, still making little forward progress is because they haven't yet come to the end of themselves. We're still trying to give orders, and interfering with God's work within us.
>
> — A. W. Tozer

Wouldn't it be a wonderful and awesome thing to live a life completely submitted to the will of God, living out of the mouth of God, and having witnesses to your loyal submission? Over the last century, submission has lost its luster and real meaning because society has watered down the essence of the word and has suggested that it shows signs of weakness and intimidation. Yet, we see in the Bible, there are countless examples in verse that shows us the significance and benefit of being able to submit to the will of God's given authority.

Hebrews 13:17 shows us, "Obey those who rule over you, and be submissive, for they watch out for your souls, as those who must give account. Let them do so with joy and not with grief, for that would be unprofitable for you." This verse indicates to us the kind of attitude that we are to have toward those who are in charge, an attitude of submission and obedience. We can only do that when we know our leaders, not before. In other words, does your conduct give your leaders reason to report joyfully about you?

We have to illustrate maturity in our walk with Christ. As believers, we must trust God that those who are over us in leadership, whether in the church, in our jobs, or in our homes, understand that God sees, owns, and rules everything, and nothing we have or ever will achieve can last without God's grace. In the Gospel of Matthew, in chapter four, we have a great example of trust and maturity in the word. We see that Jesus, who was beginning His earthly ministry, being tempted by the enemy to operate in *His* strength and will, instead of the perfect will of God. However, Jesus, being aware of the word of God and in total submission to His father, rebuffs the enemy's tricks and offers by simply standing on the word of the Lord.

Just imagine how many obstacles and failures we could avoid simply by standing and trusting in the word of the Lord. Submission is a confidence, an inner strength that can propel you towards great endeavors in life. When applied properly, it will induce major accomplishments. It is so powerful that the enemy spends a great deal of time trying to get us to walk out of character and the will of the Lord. We must allow submission and obedience to act as our GPS system, to keep us on the road of humility and meekness with the understanding that we are just a turn away traveling on that path of Destruction Boulevard.

We must never allow the enemy to cause us to walk in the spirit of arrogance or pride, for it is a dead end. Lucifer lost his place as an archangel in heaven because of his inability to deal with pride; it became toxic and turned one of God's most beautiful creatures dark and sinister. Whenever pride sets in, it causes the voice of reason to go unheard. That's why it shows God's examples about it in Proverbs 6:16, where it states: "These six *things* the Lord hates. Yes, seven *are* an abomination to Him." As we see the very first thing on the list of abominations is a proud look or "haughty eyes." Whenever a person walks in a spirit of pride and arrogance, it becomes an abomination unto God.

Jesus taught us a parable in the Gospel of Luke, in chapter eighteen, about two men who went down to the house of God. One of these men walked and trusted in his own righteousness and despised others, while the other man walked in humility and shame. Jesus said in verse fourteen, "I tell you, this man went down to his house justified *rather* than the other; for everyone who exalts himself will be humbled, and he who humbles himself will be exalted." What we can gleam from this example Jesus shares with us is that attitude determines altitude. You see that whenever pride latches onto individuals, it robs them from their ability to hear clearly. Self-righteousness is dangerous. For that reason alone, do not allow pride in your achievements to cut you off from the grace of God.

In today's culture, submission has become a lost practice. It's no wonder, as society has geared people to be loud, obnoxious, and outrageous. We watch the pundits screaming and shouting each other down on the television shows while the politicians holler and scream at each other across the aisles. Not to mention the television reality shows that exhibit no decorum at all. However, the scriptures remind us that we are to adopt the mind and attitude of our Lord and Savior, Jesus Christ, who understood His purpose and assignment and refused to allow anyone to cause Him to operate out of the will of His father.

Submission is the umbilical cord between heaven and earth, and everything in the earth's realm is operating on this system. When the disciples wanted to learn how to pray, Jesus taught them to solicit the will of God, that it be done on earth as it is in heaven. He wanted them to submit completely to God and experience His provision, wealth, and fulfillment by trusting the perfect will of God. Submission teaches us discipline and obedience. All too often, we take life for granted, going on with our days as though time is on our side. In reality, time waits for no one. We must grasp every moment, every opportunity, and make the best of it. For the Bible teaches us that every idle moment and word we waste will be judged. So we are encouraged to make the best of every second we have on this earth to be productive, progressive, and effective, to reach new heights and dimensions, to soar above the expectations of others, and to submit to God, for He knows the end from the beginning, so let us walk a life of total success and victory.

In order to walk in this realm, we must allow the Holy Spirit to take up residence inside of us, until we cease to be influenced by people whose goal is to sidetrack us from reaching our potential. It was John F. Kennedy who said, "Victory has a thousand fathers, but defeat is an orphan." Failure to submit can and will cause all sorts of consequences. Romans 13:1–2 articulates:

> Let every soul be subject to the governing authorities. For there is no authority except from God, and the authorities that exist are appointed by God. Therefore whoever resists the authority resists the ordinance of God and those who resist will bring judgment on themselves.

We see here that Jesus and His apostles never disobeyed the government for personal reasons; when they did disobey, it was because of their loyalty to the higher power. Their disobedience was not cheap; they were threatened, beaten, tortured, and thrown in jail for their convictions. Like them, if we are compelled to disobey, we must be ready to accept the consequences.

We are warned to respect those in charge and to lift them up in prayer; failure to comply will result in unfavorable ramifications for us. David was also a prime example; he was a shepherd lad who became king of Israel. David led sheep and the sheep followed, but the goat's kick, bite, and butt. When David was young, God trained him on the ways of submission and obedience. David rose to a prominent state by following the will of God through faith, obedience, and submission. Through his trust in God, he killed the giant Goliath and then received instant fame and notoriety. Many in the crowd chanted that Saul the King had killed thousands, while David killed tens of thousands.

Saul became jealous of David's impeding and increasing popularity, which led to an unsuccessful attempt on David's life by Saul. The whole time that Saul was mistreating and plotting to destroy him, David remained faithful and submitted to his leader even when he had an opportunity to kill King Saul. The times that he was near him, he allowed his respect for God to guard his heart. You and I can learn a valuable lesson here. We will never have to come against a leader who says that he is of God; however, if his leadership is of man, it will surely crumble, like King Saul's eventually did. However, if the leadership is of God, both He and it will withstand and win out over every storm, every obstacle, and every form of opposition and persecution. It will win! If we oppose that rule, we can find ourselves at odds with God.

You see, God expects us to learn from the examples of others that lived before us. Contrary to what we may have heard, our own experience is not always the best teacher. We can learn by reading the Bible and allowing the Holy Spirit of God to teach us by showing us what has happened to various people in the past. We may have different views and opinions from our leaders, but remember God doesn't like His people to come against His chosen, His anointed. God's ordained leaders may not always be right in their decisions and actions, but God has called them and placed them, so don't touch them.

We have an example in Numbers 12:1: "Then Miriam and Aaron spoke against Moses because of the Ethiopian woman whom he had married; for he had married an Ethiopian woman." Both Moses' sister and brother shared their disapproval of their brother's choice of wife, but this issue went further than that. They hated the fact that Moses was God's man for the hour. They had allowed the enemy to provoke actions of deceit among themselves. They tried to frustrate their leader because of their unwillingness to submit to leadership. Numbers 12:2–8 sheds more light on the jealousy and then the resolution when it points out:

> So they said, "Has the LORD indeed spoken only through Moses? Has He not spoken through us also?" And the LORD heard *it*. (Now the man Moses *was* very humble, more than all men who *were* on the face of the earth.) Suddenly the LORD said to Moses, Aaron, and Miriam, "Come out, you three, to the tabernacle of meeting!" So the three came out. Then the LORD came down in the pillar of cloud and stood *in* the door of the tabernacle, and called Aaron and Miriam.

And they both went forward. Then He said, "Hear now My words: If there is a prophet among you, *I,* the LORD, make Myself known to him in a vision; I speak to him in a dream. Not so with My servant Moses; He *is* faithful in all My house. I speak with him face to face, Even plainly, and not in dark sayings; And he sees the form of the LORD. Why then were you not afraid to speak against My servant Moses?"

Can you see God's attitude and demeanor toward those who come up against *His* anointed, *His* chosen one? You and I might not always agree that the person in charge of us is equipped for the job, but if He says he is called, then it's best to leave that person alone. If we can't get along, then it's better to leave than to get in trouble with the Lord. Take notice at what happened in verses nine and ten: "So the anger of the LORD was aroused against them, and He departed. And when the cloud departed from above the tabernacle, suddenly Miriam *became* leprous, as *white as* snow. Then Aaron turned toward Miriam, and there she was, a leper." Why? Because she came against God's anointed; it was like coming against God himself.

That's worth saying again: to deny and question God's anointed vessels is to oppose God himself. We must learn, too, that the straight and narrow road to God's will is much greater than the wide and destructive path that, seemingly, the majority chooses to follow. While many of us appear to receive comfort and satisfaction with the majority, it is in the minority that we see the greater rewards of success, where we can remain confident, even as others disagree with and resent us.

It is easy to look back with regret and recognize the idiocy and the nonsense of our actions. Most times it is harder to recognize the lunacy of our plans while we are carrying them out because in some way, at that moment, they seem appropriate. To omit the foolish ideas before they turn into absurd actions requires us to eradicate the wrongful thoughts and the ill intentions. Failing to do this is what caused Miriam and Aaron much grief. Aaron and Miriam resented the fact that God was using Moses more than them. These are but a few examples of refusing to acknowledge the aspect of submission and the consequences of such actions.

Aaron and Miriam resented the fact God was using Moses more than them. Questioning the judgment of God and in essence saying, "God, I'm smarter than you. You made an error by not consulting with us on this matter for your choice of a leader." On the other hand, in verses eleven and twelve, we find Aaron speaking to Moses with remorse and apologetic, "So Aaron said to Moses, "Oh, my lord! Please do not lay *this* sin on us, in which we have done foolishly and in which we have sinned. Please do not let her be as one dead, whose flesh is half consumed when he comes out of his mother's womb!" We see Miriam's horrible condition as Aaron pleads with Moses. He begged that the punishment for speaking foolishly and the sinfulness in their speech be forgiven, for he had realized that Satan hath filled their hearts with envy and malice. So Moses, who was meek and humble, cried out to the Lord for his sister, but look at God's answer in verse fourteen: "Then the Lord said to Moses, 'If her father had but spit in her face, would she not be shamed seven days? Let her be shut out of the camp seven days, and afterward she may be received *again*.'"

In other words, God was saying no to Moses. He wanted us to understand that there is a price to pay for insubordination and rejecting submission, for her repudiation was not only against man, but also against God and the very fabric of His perfect will. Actually, the punishment was quite lenient, for she would have gotten seven days for spitting in her father's face (spitting in someone's face was considered the ultimate insult); thus, we see the mercy of our God. Once again, God was merciful while maintaining an effective discipline. As believers we must understand that all good and perfect gifts come from above. We must honor those who God has placed in our life as His chosen ambassadors.

QUESTIONS FOR "SUBMISSION":

1] What role has submission or the lack of submission played concerning you fulfilling your destiny?

a] _____
_____
_____
_____

2] Do you find yourself struggling with submission in your home, church, or relationship? Explain.

a] _____
_____
_____
_____

3] What steps are you willing to take to become more submissive to the word of God concerning your life?

a] _____
_____
_____
_____

(7)

Launch Into The Deep

There will come a time when the Lord will call upon us to go into deeper waters. Like when Jesus suggested to Peter to take the boat into deeper waters. However, it is our body and minds that are the vessels and the deep waters represent our spirit and consciousness. It is there that we must launch.

God's plan for our life is that we all reach our potential that He created for us. Throughout the course of our lives He will highlight areas that we need improvement in so that we can live a victorious life. Understand that God's plan was never for us to settle or barely get by. We were designed to excel, and we also are equipped with everything we need to live abundant lives. Jeremiah 1:5 declares, "Before I formed you in the womb I knew you; before you were born I sanctified you; I ordained you a prophet to the nations." He assigned a calling on his life before he was ever conceived; his destiny was already set before his arrival.

God spoke purpose, inevitability, and circumstance—a divine decree—into Jeremiah's life. Throughout his life he is reminded of what He had deposited inside of him. As believers and children of God, we must see ourselves as champions on the inside, even if on the outside we are surrounded by negativity and faced with failure.

We must be sure to make positive confessions over our life every day, challenging the champion to rise up and receive his crown. Basically, we must get into the habit of declaring God's aspirations for us every day. In the morning as we look into the mirror, we must see purpose and destiny in us and around us.

We must value the tongue and realize the power it possesses and declare that no matter what the day brings, we will have the victory over situations in our life. In the book of Ecclesiastes, chapter nine, verse eleven, it affirms that we must be diligent. "I returned and saw under the sun that—the race *is* not to the swift, nor the battle to the strong, nor bread to the wise, nor riches to men of understanding, nor favor to men of skill; but time and chance happen to them all." It isn't hard to find cases where the swiftest or the strongest do not always win, that the intelligent are not rewarded with honor or wealth. A lot of people witness this and claim that life isn't fair. And they are right. The world is now finite, and sin has become a twisted life, making it what God had not intended for it to be. The enemy tries to reduce our expectations. The Book of Proverbs emphasizes how life would be if people acted accordingly and fairly. Ecclesiastes shows us what usually happens in this imperfect and sinful world.

Solomon reminds us that no matter how fast we try to get ahead in life, there still is a course that needs to be completed that is often beset by obstacles and many twists and turns in trying to reach that finish line. Therefore, we must be careful and methodical in our endeavor in order to fulfill the assignment designated for each of our lives. There are times when we feel like forfeiting the mission and other times we quit the mission. Because of missteps or bad judgments, we want to throw in the towel like a wounded fighter when this is the perfect time that we need to dig within, deep into ourselves, and find that extra gear, which is in there ready to kick in, and move full-steam ahead to our appointed place. Each of us, throughout the course of a day, has internal conversations and dialogue.

In fact, it is said that we talk often at times more to ourselves than we do to other people, and it's what we say that makes a difference within our consciousness. Are we challenging ourselves to reach the pinnacle that has been set for us, or are we convincing ourselves to settle to be ordinary and complacent observing from the sidelines while everybody else is in the game competing for the prize that is our birthright? We have to get into the game. Too many of us become spectators and never participate, simply because we allow one failed moment to define our whole future. We must recognize that failure should be used as a springboard that allows us to bounce back and be all that we were designed to be. Everything will not go our way. Each day will bring about inconveniences and surprises. We must make a conscientious choice to not let the bad circumstances upset us and deter us from the promises that God has for us. Please understand that there is always a light at the end of the dark tunnel. Instead of giving stress-related situations the authorization to steal our joy, we must find the positive in all things, especially when we feel as if things are not going the way we think that they should.

Romans 8:28 asserts, "And we know that all things work together for good to them that love God, to them who are the called according to *His* purpose." When we understand our purpose and calling, our adversary may wound us and even knock us down, but our resolve will never be. One of the most difficult fights we face is going to be the one within. Anyone can engage in a fight with someone that is not connected to them, but what do you do when your biggest opponent is within? How do you apprehend and beat down an enemy to whom you are connected? Imagine attacking an enemy and every blow that you lay on him causes *you* pain. You would find it difficult to continue to attack, right? Every time you swing or connect a blow, you are absorbing the brunt of true pain. How do you deny yourself from the things that are yours, in order to subdue your flesh?

Understand that God works in all things — not just in isolated situations and incidents — for our good. This does not mean that everything that we go through in life is good. Evil is prevalent in our culture and the disgraced and immoral world; however, God is able to turn every situation, every condition, every circumstance and occurrence around for our long-term good. I want you to take notice that God is not operating to make us happy, but to fulfill His purpose for us. Take heed, also, that this promise is not for everybody. It can be claimed by those who love God and are called according to His purpose. "Called" refers to those that have Christ as their Lord and Savior. For the ones that are called have a new view, a new outlook, a new attitude, and a whole new mindset on life. They trust in God and have faith in God, learning how to accept opposed to resenting the pain and persecution because God is with them.

So, for the most part, it is the issues in life that are holding us back and causing us to fail; we must be vigilant and sober. We must never lose focus and think this is all about us. We have to also appreciate the fact that our actions have direct and indirect consequences for others, too. Therefore, we must be flexible and willing to make adjustments so that we can be used mightily to carry out the assignment that is designed for each and every one of us. We must then want the things of God even more than the things that the enemy is offering in exchange for us to miss the plan for our life. We must want to be used. He's just waiting on the sidelines, trying to draw us to His team because He knows that He has to launch us into the deep with the understanding that the one person that can prevent us the will for our lives is the enemy inside of us. Many of the wars and challenges that we face are the struggles within our flesh, causing us to never "discover the champion inside of us."

Many of us want to be defined and associated with stuff and people who God has told us to abandon, wanting to carry on with that Saul spirit, which refuses to detach itself from the things that God has disdain for. Our spirit must be trained in order to be used for the Master's service, to be an asset and not a derelict. In Galatians six, we are reminded that it's not what's on the outside, but what is inside that counts. Paul's letter exclaims in verse fifteen, "For in Christ Jesus neither circumcision nor un-circumcision avails anything, but a new creation." That newness is you becoming a new you, discovering a part of you that exist already but has yet to be tapped into. Once it is discovered, we must learn and begin to discipline that old nature that would love to just sit around and do nothing and be unprofitable for the kingdom of God. The world is full of allurements and enticements that seek to deter us, and every day we are confronted by social and cultural pressures, not to mention the obvious and undisguised information that is designed specifically to mislead and persuade us to remain in darkness: propaganda.

We must prepare and develop our newness to be used for the master service, to be an asset and not a deficit. Also chapter six of Galatians, verses sixteen and seventeen essentially say, "I say then, walk in the spirit, and ye shall not fulfill the lust of the flesh." In other words, the flesh fights against the spirit, and the spirit against the flesh; because these are contrary to one another, we are prevented from doing what it is that we should be doing. When we become *born again,* we must remember that our new nature must yield to the spirit. We must make a choice to let God become our helper and guide to all truth. We must not be afraid to launch into the deep, for it is deep, but the Lord has prepared areas of abundance for all those that are willing to walk in total obedience to His holy word.

He only wants to cultivate our ways and show great and powerful things to those that will trust Him, even when they cannot see the manifestation readily. They would hold on to His promise He made with the children of Israel, and even to us today He would never leave us or forsake us. In our history we have many examples of people who overcame the obstacles and deficiencies that were placed in their paths to hinder them, and yet they conquered that which tried to prevent them from ascending to that place of prominence. Abraham Lincoln lost many elections before he became the president of the United States. Theodore Roosevelt, a near-sighted and sickly child, learned horseback riding and boxing in order to toughen himself up, and he became president. Franklin D. Roosevelt overcame the effects of polio. Helen Keller could not hear or see, but she learned to communicate. How about Winston Churchill, who failed at school but still became a great statesman and communicator? All of these individuals had to overcome their shortcomings to launch into the deep.

Too many of us often allow our past failures, our perceived faults and shortcomings, and deficiencies, to overcome our achievements and ability to succeed. We live in a society that values success, thus making it hard for many of us to handle failure, rejection, and criticism. Whenever we sense that criticism is headed our way, we clam up in a shell and try to protect ourselves from the brunt of the blow(s). All too often we allow that feeling of being alone to shield us from the eyes of the world, to be our anesthesia that would numb us from the pain of failure. So the inability to face the stares of the critics of the world keeps us locked in a cage, screaming to be accepted by the negative voices that ring in our ears with consistency.

As believers we are afforded an opportunity to witness a lesson Jesus shows us between him and his disciples in Luke 5:3–6:

> Then He got into one of the boats, which was Simon's, and asked him to put out a little from the land. And He sat down and taught the multitudes from the boat. When He had stopped speaking, He said to Simon, "Launch out into the deep and let down your nets for a catch." But Simon answered and said to Him, "Master, we have toiled all night and caught nothing; nevertheless at Your word I will let down the net." And when they had done this, they caught a great number of fish, and their net was breaking.

Peter had gone fishing with some of his fishing partners. They had been out all night long trying to catch some fish, which proved to be futile. When morning had come and frustration had set in, he began to wash his net as a sign of failure. Jesus noticed a crowd coming toward him, and He beckoned to Peter to let Him use the boat to go and launch further from the shore. Oftentimes in our lives, we tend to hang around the shores of our banks—our comfort zone, our blanket of security—afraid of experiencing the unseen things, which repeatedly hinders us from reaching our full potential.

I will never forget that as a young boy I thought I had mastered the art of swimming. I convinced myself that I was an expert, an avid swimmer that had mastered the three-foot and five-foot areas of the pool. I would practice all the latest moves and techniques of my day, racing back and forth across the pool, feeling safe and secure as long as my feet were touching the bottom of the pool. Unbeknownst to me, I was fooling nobody but myself. Those that really knew me recognized that I was an experienced swimmer only in my own mind. One day I was standing by the eight foot area and someone thought that it would be cool and funny to push me into the pool, an element with which I was unfamiliar. When I was faced with leaning on my technique, I almost drowned because I was forced out of my comfort zone.

Jesus, being omniscient, told Peter, an experienced fisherman, to launch out into the deep. Peter was reluctant at first; after all, he was the expert fisherman, and Jesus was by nature a carpenter, but after some debate and resistance, he adhered to the advice of the Lord. Peter allowed submission and obedience to kick in when stubbornness and pride wanted to rise up. When he said to Jesus, "At thy word, I will let down the net," humility and trust came into play. It was in the deep that the nets began to fragment with the weight of abundance, but as long as Peter hugged the shore, he would have continued to receive nothing. As we cease to lean away from our understanding and rely completely on His word and direction for our lives, we will open ourselves up to receive the blessings that are our true rewards. Trust and believe that God will take you from the familiar to the unfamiliar with the smoothest of transitions and grant us the opportunity to reap the rewards. We must learn from this event that has transpired. How many of us have forfeited the promise which was designed for us because of our failure to launch into the deep?

We are reminded in 2 Corinthians 4:17–18:

> For our light affliction, which is but for a moment, is working for us a far more exceeding *and* eternal weight of glory, while we do not look at the things that are seen, but at the things that are not seen. For the things that are seen *are* temporary, but the things that are not seen are eternal.

In other words, our bad situations should not overshadow our faith and disillusion us. It is easy to lose heart and give up. We all have faced situations in our personal lives, whether in a relationship or on the job, that have caused us to be stagnant or simply just want to quit. We have to understand and realize that there is a purpose in our suffering. It is at that moment that God is working on us. We must understand that pressure can make or break us. The thing that separates a black coal from a diamond is the amount of pressure that it endures.

When adversity and challenges come our way, the main distinction that appears to stand out particularly from winning and appearing in the loss column is how you are playing the game. A key component of paying attention will lead to success. One thing is for certain: if you continue to do nothing and always stand back, you cannot expect to win or even achieve anything in this life. At every juncture we are given, we must take full advantage of that opportunity while refusing to settle for less, all the while striving to be all that we can be, even when it means stepping away from our comfort zone. Do not become attached to complacency and normalcy; continue to excel at every opportunity that is offered to us. Remember that the power to reach our God-given purpose lies deep within us. *Do not settle!*

QUESTIONS FOR "LAUNCH INTO THE DEEP":

1] What specific area in your life have you become dormant? Explain.

a] _____
_____
_____
_____

2] For a few moments think about what God has called for you to do. Ask yourself: have you obeyed the voice of God? If not, explain why. If yes, show results.

a] _____
_____
_____
_____

(8)
Preparing to take off

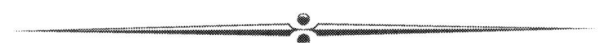

The largest opponent of courage is fear.

Fear of the unknown.

Fear of failure.

Fear of others and what they think of us.

Successful people acknowledge fears, but work to conquer them.

Rudyard Kipling

Imagine for a minute being on an airplane for the very first time in your life. As you get on the plane, there is a lot of movement: passengers getting settled in their seats, flight attendants are moving about making sure that everybody and everything is in order and in its place. You're feeling a sense of anxiety as the chaotic atmosphere plays itself out around you. Your heart is racing a hundred miles an hour. The nervousness and anxiousness are building within, when finally and abruptly you hear this voice come across the intercom: "Ladies and gentleman, this is your captain speaking. We'd like to welcome you onboard International Airlines for our trip to Australia. Duration of our flight will be fifteen hours. We are experiencing beautiful weather, so we can anticipate a fairly smooth and comfortable flight today. Once again we want to thank you for choosing to fly with us today and we hope that you enjoy your flight."

Suddenly, all your fears and anxiety begin to subside when you hear that stern yet calm voice that reassures you that he is in charge and that there is nothing to worry about. Many times in our lives, the greatest dilemma that stands in the way of our success is the fear to take that flight to our destiny. Fear will have a hold on you like a terrorist that steals our joy and controls and alters our movements each and every day. It will have us looking over our shoulders wondering whether or not we will be attacked as it sabotages our opportunity to grow and expand. We succumb to a substandard existence of mediocrity that involves complaining and blaming everyone and everything for our lack of progress.

We become comfortable in the waddling of complacency, feeling trapped and helpless, while reaching out for the sympathizers who will rally to our cause, staying bitter and angry as a justification for our decision to settle. How foolish is that? This type of mindset and attitude hinders us from reaching that plateau that has been pre-destined by God for all of us in our life. To dwell on your problems more than trusting in God will keep you handcuffed to a state of complaining and ultimately failure. Psychologists and researchers who have studied "hope theory" have found that those who tend to focus on a solution rather than dwell on the problems increase their capacity to reach their goals, and in the process their spirits are uplifted.

Therefore we must build up our immune system. Just as our physical immune system can become weakened, so too can our spiritual immune system be weakened or strengthened. It is imperative to keep our spirit out of those dark and lonely alleys of despair and instead introduce it to the illuminated streets of hope and prosperity. We have to continue to hurdle every obstacle that life throws our way and not allow the missteps of a failed endeavor to keep us sidelined in the important races in our lives. We must keep it moving, despite the naysayers we will encounter in life. Once we get the hang of the rhythm of life, then we can make more synchronized steps in reaching our destiny.

Is it human nature that people will all too often move to the rhythm of other people and become fixated, letting other people characterize them and forfeiting the promises God has made to us? This lack of discipline will cause us to always lag back a step or two, tasting the dust of others in our mouth, when we could have been further ahead than we are if we had only moved to the beat that has been orchestrated for us by God. First Corinthians 2:9–12 states:

> But as it is written: "Eye has not seen, nor ear heard, nor have entered into the heart of man the things which God has prepared for those who love Him. But God has revealed *them* to us through His Spirit. For the Spirit searches all things, yes, the deep things of God. For what man knows the things of a man except the spirit of the man which is in him? Even so no one knows the things of God except the Spirit of God. Now we have received, not the spirit of the world, but the Spirit who is from God, that we might know the things that have been freely given to us by God."

We cannot imagine all that God has in store for us. As people of destiny, we must not allow the narrow scope of others to cause us to miss the bigger picture, when in fact the scripture that we just read alluded to the case in point and that is: the purpose that has been carved out for us is far greater than we could ever imagine. Our purpose is God-driven and cannot possibly be man-made. It requires a steady dose of His strength and guidance in order to flourish and be relevant. Even when you're faced with adversities that look like stumbling blocks, you cannot shy away from them. We must embrace every challenge as an opportunity to allow God to get the glory out of our circumstance(s). You have to have a made-up mind that says, "No matter how long it takes, I'm going to trust God every step of the way."

By allowing our challenges to serve as the catalyst to spark and ignite creativity and innovation, we can then begin to produce life-changing results. Therefore, we must not allow the cares and pressures of the world to crowd out the promises of God. We must be steadfast in our resolve. Too often we allow failure and disappointment to weigh us down, causing us to loiter in disarray, grasping for life support from unauthorized sources. Because we are equipped with the ability to be introspective, we must rely on our predisposition to excel and rise above the fray of opposition, hunker down, and move full speed ahead to the point of our destiny, all the while embracing the speed bumps. Just remember, you were chosen for this course; it was designed specially and specifically for you.

You have to adopt a conscientious perspective that "this is my season" to excel in everything that God has instructed me to do, with the understanding that there will be slip-ups, mistakes, and sometimes setbacks, but never regrets. You cannot allow the enemy to cause a survival mentality of settling for less, thinking that as long as you have a little bit left, that everything is going to be all right. No, you are a winner that lives and cherishes the promises of God, accepting His word to be true, esteeming them above everything else. No matter how difficult, no matter how unfair life will appear, you will do more than just maintain. Go forward with the confidence in the fact that He called you for this position. Philippians 1:6 emphasizes, "being confident of this very thing, that He who has begun a good work in you will complete *it* until the day of Jesus Christ."

Yes, sometimes you feel as though you aren't making progress, where nothing works. Try as you might to get to that next level, it just feels as if all of our efforts are proven to be futile. In the workplace, especially, we feel this play out. After a series of newcomers enter and pass us for promotions, our dreams to reach or break the ceiling flutters away. Suddenly, it feels as if we are grounded while looking at others soaring to new heights, breaking the ceiling that we once saw ourselves doing. However, if we don't let bitterness overtake us and are willing to tweak a few things, by not letting frustration get the best of us or past disappointments preoccupy our mental state, then we can glean a new perspective that can and will improve our overall performance, which will then ignite our mission and allow us to soar to new levels.

When you are discouraged, remember that God won't give up on you. As with the Philippians, God will help you to grow in grace until He has completed His work in your life. He promises to finish the work He has begun. Don't let your present condition defraud you of knowing who He is and what He means to your life. Just remember God's promise and provision whenever you feel incomplete, unfinished, or distressed by your imperfection and deficiencies. When God starts a project, He finishes it.

Take heed in the lessons that are shown in Hebrews 10:35–38:

> Therefore do not cast away your confidence, which has great reward. For you have need of endurance, so that after you have done the will of God, you may receive the promise: "For yet a little while, *And* He who is coming will come and will not tarry. Now the just shall live by faith; but if *anyone* draws back, My soul has no pleasure in him."

In other words, we are encouraged not to abandon our faith in the hardest of times, but to show by our perseverance that our faith is real. We don't usually feel that suffering is good for us, but it can build patience in us, which leads to character.

Did you know that it took Thomas Edison several years to develop the first commercially feasible electric light bulb? What if Thomas Edison had become frustrated by his failed attempts to bring forth that which he had envisioned in his mind? In 1923, Robert Woodruff, who served as president of Coca-Cola until 1955, had a bold vision that every American serviceman be given the opportunity to taste his Coca-Cola product for five cents, no matter what it would cost his company. It was a costly and lofty vision that lost the company a lot of money at first but paid off in the end. Instead of tanking, Coca-Cola turned things around into huge profits. Still today Coca-Cola remains a profitable mainstay in our cultural fabric. Visionaries are willing to hold onto their visions no matter what failure or hiccups may come their way. They understand that success is usually wrapped and packaged in frustration, inadequate moments, defeat, and a whole slew of obstacles that can thwart a dream, but they also recognize that patience is a virtue every great visionary must possess.

Therefore, it is imperative that we embrace the fact that failing will be a part of life and an intricate part of being successful, because people that have a date with destiny never take failure as a personal endeavor. They use failures as a form of motivation that will inspire them to reach new heights and greater enterprises and undertakings, excelling beyond their own expectations. Paul teaches us in Hebrews not to expect instant gratification. All too often if we look for things right away, always expecting immediate results. That is not how life works for the most part. When we expect that is how life operates, then we grow impatient and toss away dreams and opportunity. The inability to navigate through the tough times, the choppy and stormy weathers, can prove to be deadly and dangerous for any endeavor, whether it is a marriage, a job, a friendship, or even a church.

Leaders and appointed people, whether over a large corporation or head of the household, have to take into account the vicissitudes, the ebb and flow that will inevitably take place in this thing called life. It is vital to the maintenance of one's stability and viability for longevity. Richard L. Evans once said, "It isn't always other[s] that enslave us. Sometimes we let circumstance enslave us; sometimes we let routine enslave us; sometimes we let things enslave us. Sometimes, with weak wills, we enslave ourselves."

We all remember the brothers that were born in Ohio by the names of Orville and Wilbur Wright. They were successful entrepreneurs who had tried their hands in many ventures. Orville, while in school, had begun a printing business with a homemade press. Later, with the help of his brother, they founded and opened a weekly newspaper. After a few years they opened up a bicycle sales and repair shop in 1892, and in late 1895, the Wrights began to make preparations to manufacture their own bicycles. They introduced the "Van Cleve" on April 24, 1896; however, by 1899 there was a change in their ambitions when they turned their sights to the dynamics of aeronautics. This passion led them to contact the Smithsonian Institute in Washington, D.C. to gather information about efforts that were made by other experimenters. In just a few years' time, Orville and Wilbur Wright had gone from journalists to bicycle shop owners to bicycle manufacturers to pursuing their passion: flying. Now, whether it was a life-long goal or not, they went on to invent an aircraft in which humans could travel.

In 1900 through 1901, the Wright brothers made many attempts to get their project up and running. They first experimented with five-foot bi-plane kites, testing out man-carrying gliders on the sand dunes near Kitty Hawk. The brothers tried desperately to get a successful aircraft built. They researched the works of others that tried in this field of aerodynamics, experimenters such as S.P. Langley, a pioneer of aviation, and Otto Lilienthal, a German pioneer of aviation who, with the help of his brother Gustav, became known as "The Glider King". He was the first person to make well documented, repeated, successful, gliding flights. Orville and Wilbur studied and viewed the calculations and timetables. They decided that the previous easels were not correct. They then went on a search to find the perfect shapes. Scouring over two hundred different types and shapes that would be adequate based upon the air pressure and the curved surfaces, they finally made a choice and then devised a plan for the steering and balancing of the aircraft.

Eventually, feeling confident that their model was ready to take on new heights, the brothers must have felt a sense of release; the moment that they had been waiting for (to defy the odds of mankind) had finally arrived. They sailed off with great expectations, but to their dismay, it only lasted twelve seconds at one hundred and twenty feet. Although they were filled with frustration and disappointment, they did not give up. They gathered their previous calculations and information and went back to the drawing board. They were not in denial about their failed attempt. They looked at it as simply a setback.

We allow temporary setbacks and miscalculations to alter our purpose in life repeatedly, feeling as though we are constantly confronting an all-or-nothing situation. This is the type of attitude that causes many of us to give up and retire our progress prematurely. Wilbur and Orville would have no parts of that defeatist notion. They went back and attacked their dream with vigor and tenacity, knowing that walking away was not an option. They built a new glider and went back to Kitty Hawk in August of 1902. It was a much-improved version that yielded better results, surpassing all earlier attempts for the glider flights. With a distance of over six hundred feet, in just a few months they had tripled their distance, but they were not quite satisfied with their accomplishment.

They returned to Dayton and build a self-powered airplane with a twelve-horsepower gasoline engine with propellers that was advanced in design and efficiency that weighed seven hundred and fifty pounds. What started out as a passion had turned into a reality because of their resolve and willingness. We see that all the trials and tests had come to reveal and build the true character in these brothers. The Wright brothers held steadfast on the idea that what they had set out to do and would not be denied. Then in 1905, on a field that was near Dayton, they took a flight that lasted thirty-eight minutes and covered over thirty-eight miles. This achievement would then be culminated when they received a patent covering the pattern and design.

When obstacles and negative events challenge our lives, we must be willing to fight instead of throwing in the towel. We must be willing to fight with everything in us, down to the core. We must be willing to launch into the deep and with a determined mind, we shall be standing in the end. Remember, it's time to go to the next level: prepare to take off and see all the wondrous things that you thought were not available to you before. You are an eagle, not a chicken. Eagles are graced with keen and exceptional eyesight, powerful wings, and strong bodies—able to soar in some of the most disastrous predicaments. You embody the attributes of this beautiful creature, so prepare to take off toward your purpose, your goals, and your visions with confidence and the belief that this is your season. Soar!

Do not give the failures of yesterday authorization to ground your flight with destiny. You have to remember that you are equipped to handle whatever may come your way—good and bad. Continue to lift your head high and stay focused on the promises of God, knowing that He will sustain you. In your efforts to reach that place that you know was designed for you, dig deep. "Can't" does not exist in your vocabulary, nor does it live in your spirit. You are a by-product of Philippians 4:13, "I can do all things through Christ who strengthens me." Can we really do everything? The power that we obtain in accordance with Christ is sufficient to do His will and to confront the challenges that will arise from our commitment to doing it. As we vie for the faith, we will face troubles, pressures, and trials. When they appear, ask Christ to strengthen you.

Face every challenge with dignity and pride, knowing that the Lord is on your side, taking comfort in knowing that we have His promise and His word that He will never leave us or forsake us. For that reason we must not panic when failure comes; we must have the resolve of a super-ball that skyrockets upward with every bounce. We must embrace our Academy Award–winning performance as well as our blooper reel, understanding that balance is the key to maintaining a successful and fulfilling life. Living outside the walls and opinions of others will assure your staying power. Remember that when you look in the mirror, you only have to ask yourself one question: "Have I done my best?"

When doubt and fear come in and take up space for free, serve them their eviction notices. "Rejoice in the Lord always, and again I say, Rejoice." Let your moderation be known to all men that the Lord is at hand. Be careful for nothing, but in everything by prayer and supplication with thanksgiving. Let your request be made known unto God. The peace of God, which passeth all understanding, shall keep your hearts and mind through Christ Jesus.

Philippians 4:8 asserts:

Finally, brethren, whatever things are true, whatever things *are* noble, whatever things *are* just, whatever things *are* pure, whatever things *are* lovely, whatever things *are* of good report, if *there is* any virtue and if *there is* anything praiseworthy—meditate on these things.

What we put into our minds determines what comes out in our words and actions. Just remember, you're about to take off.

QUESTIONS FOR "PREPARING TO TAKE FLIGHT":

1] What issues have deterred you from taking flight in order to reach your destiny?

a] _____
   _____
   _____
   _____

2] Upon identifying your issues that have kept you grounded, what key things can you do to prepare yourself to overcome these issues?

a] _____
   _____
   _____
   _____

(9)

THINKING OUTSIDE THE BOX

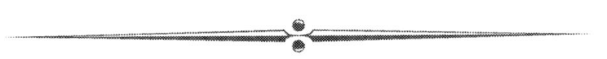

The gift of imagination is at the core of your ability to be innovative. Imagination is more important than knowledge.
Albert Einstein

God never intended us to be average or insignificant. He created us in His image and likeness to do great and mighty things. We have to remember that we are a product of who He is. He has equipped us with not only the ability to have and enjoy a long and productive life, but He has readied us for the abundance and greatness that we sometimes think that we are not prepared. We were designed to dream and be creative, make choices, and bring glory to His name. He called us the apple of His eye while placing the seed of greatness inside each and every one of us and giving us His Holy Spirit that would serve as a GPS navigation system for our lives.

It was this promise that Jesus made to His disciples when He knew His departure was inevitable. He wanted to equip them with everything that they would need to be successful in fulfilling their God-given assignments, for which they were created. In the following text we learn that Jesus had an important assignment. In John 16:7–13 we are shown:

Nevertheless I tell you the truth. It is to your advantage that I go away; for if I do not go away, the Helper will not come to you; but if I depart, I will send Him to you. And when He has come, He will convict the world of sin, and of righteousness, and of judgment: of sin, because they do not believe in Me; of righteousness, because I go to My Father and you see Me no more; of judgment, because the ruler of this world is judged. "I still have many things to say to you, but you cannot bear *them* now. However, when He, the Spirit of truth, has come, He will guide you into all truth; for He will not speak on His own *authority,* but whatever He hears He will speak; and He will tell you things to come."

God has bestowed upon each and every one of us a plan, a task to fulfill. He has provided the resources to execute and implement great works for Him. One of our assignments was and is to be fruitful and multiply, replenish the earth, to subdue and have dominion over the earth. We were not placed here to fail, to be misfits, or to sit back and allow life to pull us along a path of oppression, injustice, misery, mistakenness, laziness, and negativity to occupy a poverty-stricken mindset.

No, we are His chosen ambassadors of earth, declaring His sovereignty and walking in the newness of providence. His! Providing salt to an unseasoned nation, we as believers bear a great responsibility to provide a continued positive and effective light of our judge and master. Too many of us today forfeit our ability to do wonderful things because of our inability to defy the odds we're up against. We have to understand that when we cease to be unique and settle for being common, our impact becomes weakened; our strength and resolve fall by the wayside, culminating in our irrelevancy.

When we permit the myopic views of single-minded people to thwart our progress, that negative impact can also have a detrimental influence on the people that stand on our side. In order to leave an impression on any significant work or endeavor that you are engaged in, you must be willing to defy the ideology of the naysayers and think outside of the box to sustain optimum success. Remember that the praises of other people are not needed in order to accomplish major goals. True and lasting self-worth must *never* be contingent on whether or not people understand and stand in accordance with your work. No, my brothers and sisters, we must be willing to go at it alone many times in order to reach that plateau. Exuberant, exciting, and fun would best describe how thinking outside the box could be.

The apostle Paul was a man born out of season who was not one of the original twelve disciples that walked with Jesus. In fact, Paul was a devoted religious man who sat on the prestigious board of the Sanhedrin Council, and was as orthodox and structured as they come. The Sanhedrin was the supreme council (or court) in ancient Israel. Paul was a staunch opponent of Christianity. When his name was Saul, he persecuted Christians for their refusal to stay mainstream and conventional. He participated in the stoning of Stephen, one of the early Christian martyrs. Saul hated anything that opposed his belief. Nevertheless, one day he was knocked off of his beast and blinded by a great light. The ride that he was taking near Damascus became a ride to remember, as it was the time of transformation.

In Acts 9:3–8 we learn of Saul's conversion when it states:

> As he journeyed he came near Damascus, and suddenly a light shone around him from heaven. Then he fell to the ground, and heard a voice saying to him, "Saul, Saul, why

are you persecuting Me?" And he said, "Who are You, Lord?" Then the Lord said, "I am Jesus, whom you are persecuting. It *is* hard for you to kick against the goads." So he, trembling and astonished, said, "Lord, what do You want me to do?" Then the Lord *said* to him, "Arise and go into the city, and you will be told what you must do." And the men who journeyed with him stood speechless, hearing a voice but seeing no one. Then Saul arose from the ground, and when his eyes were opened he saw no one. But they led him by the hand and brought *him* into Damascus.

God had converted Saul into the Apostle Paul, who would then go on to become one of the most prolific New Testament writers of the Epistle. Paul had overcome great adversarial intentions once he discovered that God had other plans for his life.

His thinking had changed. He had a new found purpose. In one of his great oratories shown in Philippians 1:21–24 he says:

> For to me, to live *is* Christ, and to die *is* gain. But if *I* live on in the flesh, this *will mean* fruit from *my* labor; yet what I shall choose I cannot tell. For I am hard-pressed between the two, having a desire to depart and be with Christ, *which is* far better. Nevertheless to remain in the flesh *is* more needful for you.

It was truly unconventional at the time and totally out of the box. Paul had discovered his purpose for living while he served the Philippians and others. That purpose was to speak out boldly for Christ and to become more like Him. Thus, Paul could confidently say that dying would be even better than living, because in death he would be removed from worldly troubles.

There were other great men, such as Leonardo da Vinci, who, while well known universally for his artistic greatest (*Mona Lisa* and *The Last Supper*), also had to overcome personal issues and struggles. He too would discover that he needed to think outside of the box of conventionality. He was moody, restless, suffered from anxiety, never satisfied with his work, forever blaming himself, and believe it or not, for a period of time, he was an underachiever.

Yet, he prevailed and didn't let these hang-ups hinder him. Besides being an artist, Leonardo was also an engineer, a musician, an architect, cartographer, and a mathematician, as well as an astronomer, a botanist, zoologist, geologist, and a physiologist. He was a man of many talents that permitted him to dwell at the level of extraordinary. Many historians have suggested that Leonardo da Vinci was the most gifted man that ever lived. Leonardo presumed that he was capable of understanding all things. Because of his great artistic abilities, many of his accomplishments were overshadowed. Did you know that before Copernicus, it was da Vinci that noted that the sun did not revolve around the earth? He was also the first to suggest that the earth was a star just like the moon. He pioneered optics, hydraulics, the physics of sound, and the nature of light. He understood that sound moved in waves and concluded that light traveled faster than sound. His fascination of water motivated him to create the frogman diving suit and the snorkel. He was instrumental in the building and designing of all the canals around the city of Milan.

As you see, we can learn from da Vinci to not be one-dimensional. We must allow God to develop us and help us to uncover all of the gifts that are buried deep inside of us. We must move to our God-given destiny and not permit tension and dissatisfaction to sidetrack us from being all that we can be. This will require us to reprogram, recondition, and modify our attitudes and minds, along with challenging ourselves to not be victimized by past mistakes and failures, and then embrace our weaknesses in order to grab ahold of our purpose in life, never looking back. What we must realize is that everything in life has an expiration date on it, and it is how we operate within that time frame that determines our success.

In Ecclesiastes 3:1–8 we are reminded that everything has a time when it asserts,

> "To everything *there is* a season,
> A time for every purpose under heaven:
> A time to be born,
> And a time to die;
> A time to plant,
> And a time to pluck *what is* planted;
> A time to kill,
> And a time to heal;
> A time to break down,
> And a time to build up;
> A time to weep,
> And a time to laugh;
> A time to mourn,
> And a time to dance;
> A time to cast away stones,
> And a time to gather stones;
> A time to embrace,
> And a time to refrain from embracing;
> A time to gain,
> And a time to lose;
> A time to keep,
> And a time to throw away;
> A time to tear,
> And a time to sew;
> A time to keep silence,
> And a time to speak;
> A time to love,
> And a time to hate;
> A time of war,
> And a time of peace.

It is vitally important that you recognize your season, for this will be beneficial for the production of your harvest, which will cause your life to overflow with the goodness of the Lord. The failure to operate in your season is one of the main reasons that will cause you to miss the great opportunities that were available to you. Just imagine drinking milk or eating something that has expired. It can cause great discomfort, pain, or even fatality simply because we didn't take advantage of the time before it expired. This basic principle can save you from enduring many headaches, agony, and mental suffering, along with various setbacks.

Having the fortitude to operate within the window of opportunity that's provided enhances the freshness of creativity and the effectiveness of your work(s). Rediscover your sense of divine purpose and hone in on your destiny. Find the things inside of you that will motivate you, that excite you. We all have talents and hidden riches within to uncover. Begin the process by asking some pertinent questions, such as: what am I passionate about? What do I love doing? What can I contribute? Recognize that the answers to these questions can catapult you on your way to greatness by achieving everything you put your mind to and accomplish.

Thinking outside the box essentially means to not be mainstream or conventional when you start to incorporate your plans for greatness. Remember that the Bible says He will give us the desires of our hearts. We must reach outside of ourselves, enlarge our circle with like-minded individuals, and then press forward without hesitation or apprehension. Plan your work and work your plan, taking advantage of your season. Be aggressive and deliberate when maximizing that window of opportunity in your life. Let the doubters and the negativity of others be the fuel that ignites and drives your vision and passion. Then you can look in the mirror at the end of a day and with your best Frank Sinatra impression, say or sing, "I did it my way."

Matthew 16:13–17 says:

> When Jesus came into the region of Caesarea Philippi, He asked His disciples, saying, "Who do men say that I, the Son of Man, am?" So they said, "Some *say* John the Baptist, some Elijah, and others Jeremiah or one of the prophets." He said to them, "But who do you say that I am?" Simon Peter answered and said, "You are the Christ, the Son of the living God." Jesus answered and said to him, "Blessed are you, Simon Bar-Jonah, for flesh and blood has not revealed *this* to you, but My Father who is in heaven."

In his day, Jesus was a controversial figure. Many of the religious and traditional thinkers of that time had a problem with His approach to things. His earthly pedigree was not up to par for all of his critics. His methods caused many to question His authenticity, calling Him the Son of Beelzebub.

However, Jesus did not permit the opinions of men to discourage him from doing great work; He continued to operate in His gift and calling. Imagine if you were given an assignment you had only a short amount of time to fulfill. Wouldn't you search and look for the best means to ensure that you would have the best opportunity to achieve your goal(s)? This was the mandate placed on the life of Jesus Christ, to bring a dying generation back to a loving Father, serving as a mediator for all mankind. With an expiration date of three-and-a-half years, he had to make every second count. Now most people would have sought out those that were well versed and enameled in their fields of expertise to aid him in accomplishing His mission.

Jesus did the total opposite: He chose novices, men that had no experience and lacked the proficiency in the areas that were needed to assist him in his task. No, He didn't go to the synagogue and choose men with theological knowledge, nor did He bother with the Pharisees or scribes, nor did He seek men of the Sanhedrin Council. Instead, He chose fishermen to assist Him in His mission. Jesus embraced the fact that He was being alienated by the mainstream religious sector, and He stepped outside the box as He presented the heart of our God. All the while, He taught us the true meaning of the words of his Father, bringing clarity and simplicity to the task that was given to Him. He transformed the minds of men, who society had deemed unlearned and ignorant, empowering them to do great and mighty endeavors.

We must understand that God's power shows up in our weakest moments when we are not as convinced of our situations; when we are weak, He is strong. I believe that He allows us weakness so that we can lean on him, for power is a magnet to weakness. Sometimes our struggles are a divine provision or arrangement served to us by God to open up our minds and consciousness to a wealth of opportunity that would have never been revealed. Instead of running and complaining about the challenges that we may face in our lives, we must confront them head-on with a certain degree of confidence and certainty, that no matter what that challenge may bring, we will overcome them.

Even though we are at different levels of maturity in our journey with the Lord, we must remain steadfast in our resolve and appreciate the fact that He will not put more on us than we are able to bear. Let the trials and struggles show us what areas we need improvement and then make a conscious effort to improve them. The people that are driven don't have time to be sidetracked by people with narcissistic intentions. When you are on a mission that needs to be done in a timely fashion, this is the type of assignment that you have to "keep it moving". You cannot allow inconsistent, half-hearted thrill seekers to tag along, as we will learn from the following text found in Luke 9:57–62:

> Now it happened as they journeyed on the road, *that* someone said to Him, "Lord, I will follow You wherever You go." And Jesus said to him, "Foxes have holes and birds of the air *have* nests, but the Son of Man has nowhere to lay *His* head." Then He said to another, "Follow Me." But he said, "Lord, let me first go and bury my father." Jesus said to him, "Let the dead bury their own dead, but you go and preach the kingdom of God." And another also said, "Lord, I will follow You, but let me first go *and* bid them farewell who are at my house." But Jesus said to him, "No one, having put his hand to the plow, and looking back, is fit for the kingdom of God."

Total dedication was needed, not a half-hearted commitment; they couldn't pick or choose among Jesus' ideas and follow him selectively. We must be willing to accept the cross along with the crown, judgment as well as mercy. We must be able to think outside of that box of generality and count up the cost and be willing to abandon everything that has given us security. By staying focused, we should allow nothing to distract us from the manner of living that He calls good and true. That is what is needed to tackle our goals and reach the awaiting plateaus in our lives.

Bishop T.D. Jakes asked the question, "What do the giraffe and turtle have in common? Absolutely nothing!" While the giraffe, whose stature often reaches heights of some eighteen feet and eats off the tree limbs in high places, the turtle has a different view—a grounded perspective. Many of us will entangle and align ourselves with those people of totally different levels of thinking. Now while their methods may work for them, always doubtful and singing negative tunes every time we come across them, it does nothing in our quest to achieve. Those types of negative vibes can and will prove detrimental to a mover and shaker that entertains such company.

That is why it is imperative not to attach ourselves to anything that is unequally yoked. Therefore, we must surround ourselves with those traveling in the same direction we are headed. Conversely, we are to find someone who has traveled that road before, being enthusiastic in seeking his or her experiences and advice to attain our God-given assignment. Drown out and smother the voices of simple-minded, misguided individuals who assume that without them in your life, you cannot reach your destiny and purpose.

Never give up your dreams and passions. Proceed with the knowledge of what the great generals understood, which is, every now and then they may lose a battle or two, but they stay encouraged, knowing that their missteps and miscalculations only serve as a measuring stick for the bigger picture, which is the war. Just as in life, in order to live outside of the box, you must be willing to not only experience the setbacks and some obstacles, you must be willing to confront them. As we all know, games are known to have peaks and valleys, one quarter doesn't earn you a victory or a championship. It requires at least three quarters and a better-than-even quarter, or a string of four good quarters.

Whether it's fair or not, seen or unseen, our focus must not change or wander, for we are as arrows are in the hands of a mighty archer, aimed and pointed to reach new heights above our limited understanding of life. It would be foolish of us to try to fit God into our mold, making His plans and purposes conform to ours. Instead it is up to us to strive to fit into His plans, for He had greater understanding of where our lanes are. We learn this in Isaiah 55:8–12:

> "For My thoughts *are* not your thoughts, nor *are* your ways My ways," says the LORD. "For *as* the heavens are higher than the earth, so are My ways higher than your ways, and My thoughts than your thoughts. "For as the rain comes down, and the snow from heaven, and do not return there, but water the earth, and make it bring forth and bud, that it may give seed to the sower and bread to the eater, so shall My word be that goes forth from My mouth; it shall not return to Me void, but it shall accomplish what I please, and it shall prosper *in the thing* for which I sent it. For you shall go out with joy, and be led out with peace; the mountains and the hills shall break forth into singing before you, and all the trees of the field shall clap *their* hands."

Remember, God is in control; He's got this. Just cast your cares upon Him, step back, stand still, and let Him handle your adversaries, enemies, haters, and all the well-wishers that are hoping for your demise. Also remember: greater is He who is inside of you, than he that is in this world. You are a conqueror, so think outside the box.

QUESTIONS FOR "THINKING OUTSIDE THE BOX":

1] What qualities or characteristics do you think set you apart from others?

a] _____
_____
_____
_____

2] Are you connected to people that motivate you or people that constantly pull from you? Explain.

a] _____
_____
_____
_____

(10)

STRETCHING FOR THE FINISH LINE

Vision helps us to see the possibilities of tomorrow within the realities of today and motivates us to do what is needed to be done. Dreams are extremely important. You can't do it unless you can imagine it.

George Lucas

First Corinthians 9:24–27:

Do you not know that those who run in a race all run, but one receives the prize? Run in such a way that you may obtain *it*. And everyone who competes *for the prize* is temperate in all things. Now they *do it* to obtain a perishable crown, but we *for* an imperishable *crown.* Therefore I run thus: not with uncertainty. Thus I fight: not as *one who* beats the air. But I discipline my body and bring *it* into subjection, lest, when I have preached to others, I myself should become disqualified.

Strive for that crown!

Imagine going out one Saturday afternoon to watch your local track team race the four hundred or the eight hundred meter event for the first time. You will probably notice that the runners are not lined up in an even line at the starting mark. Instead, what you will see is that the runners, although in their lanes, are starting at staggered positions. The reason that they are staggered is to ensure that each runner covers equal distance. If they were lined straight across at the start, then that would mean the runners on the outside lanes are traveling a greater distance to reach the goal line. From a novice's perspective, it may appear that it is an unfair advantage to some of the runners, but the judges know that during the course of the race that the distance will balance itself out.

Sometimes in life we tend to look at where other people have started out and what they have is a feeling of disservice and that the playing field is against them. However, heed must be taken to the runners and learn a lesson from their stance and disposition, which is to stay in our lanes and run the course as it has been set out for us. It is vitally important that each runner stay in their own lane, for to cross over into the next person's lane is grounds for disqualification. Equally important, we must learn how to run the race that has been given us with patience, discipline, and perseverance and at the same time have the presence of mind to understand that the enemy's plan and desire is to thwart your efforts in completing the course that God has mapped out for us. Satan would rather we quit mid-stream and settle for being mediocre, feeling sorry for ourselves and wallowing in a state of depression. So, he uses the same obstacles and hurdles to sidetrack us because he knows that as long as we stay on course, we are a threat to his kingdom. Yes, he would rather see us forfeit the prize.

Stepping up to the challenge with a display of courage will enable us to defy the odds that we find ourselves up against, regardless of what they may be. In 1936, at the Olympic games in Berlin, Germany, Jesse Owens was poised to win the long jump, an event that he had set the record for the year before by jumping twenty-six feet, eight and a quarter inches. Well, on his first jump,

Jesse inadvertently leaped and took off several inches beyond the takeoff board, resulting in a foul. His second attempt had the same outcome. With one foul away from having his dreams crushed and all of his hard work about to go down the drain, he gathered himself together. He blocked out the sight of his opponent: a tall, blue-eyed, blonde German, who stood above him in stature. He put aside the fact that Hitler and his Nazi cronies had desires to prove Aryan superiority over the blacks. Jesse launched deep within and proceeded to set an Olympic record and collected four gold medals because he refused to allow the obstacles and negativity to be a distraction to him.

We soon understand that we're not the only ones that struggle. Hebrews 12:1–3 points out:

> Wherefore seeing we also are compassed about with so great a cloud of witnesses, let us lay aside every weight, and the sin which doth so easily beset us, and let us run with patience the race that is set before us, looking unto Jesus the author and finisher of our faith; who for the joy that was set before him endured the cross, despising the shame, and is set down at the right hand of the throne of God. For consider him that endured such contradiction of sinners against himself, lest ye be wearied and faint in your minds.

This passage shows us a variety of lessons that should guide us; namely we must be willing to lay aside some of the baggage that we carry with us in this life. Also, we do not struggle alone and are not the first to wrestle with the problems we face. Others have run this race and won, and the fact that they bear witness should stir and motivate us to compete and win, too. We must not allow foolish mistakes and situations to weigh us down so we become stagnant. We must continue forward with a newfound passion and hope, fighting against all odds. Wake up each morning reviewing the areas in our life that we need to make improvement in and celebrate the areas that God is working on. We must remember that every lap we run is one less lap for those that chase after us; every day stay faithful and with the confidence that God is your protection.

Your resolve becomes stronger and stronger knowing that your test and obstacles are storing up blessings for your future. That is why we must run this race with patience, setting our focus on Jesus, who is the author of faith. Allow His perfect peace to soothe and comfort us in times of trouble. We have to start focusing on the divine destiny and take measures that will welcome the desires God has placed in our hearts to come to pass. We should then be compelled to become better stewards of our time and opportunities. H. Jackson Brown Jr. once wrote, "Don't say you don't have enough time. You have exactly the same number of hours per day that were given to Helen Keller, Louis Pasteur, Michelangelo, Mother Theresa, Leonardo da Vinci, Thomas Jefferson, and Albert Einstein."

As Christians we must be prudent and careful with how we utilize our precious time that is afforded to us. We should learn how to balance and maximize this gift in order to run a successful and effective race with as few mistakes as possible. People that make use of time management wisely achieve a great deal more than those that waste their time being idle and ineffective. Unfortunately many of us get stuck by the influence of outside distractions and fail to qualify and complete the course we were created for, becoming mere spectators watching the event that they should have been a part of. But we permit the chorus of negativity to drown out the voices of reason, leaving us limping on the sidelines injured by criticism.

We should never entertain nor envy evil people or circumstances in our lives. We are cautioned in Psalm 37:1–5:

> Do not fret because of evildoers, nor be envious of the workers of iniquity. For they shall soon be cut down like the grass, and wither as the green herb. Trust in the Lord, and do good; dwell in the land, and feed on His faithfulness. Delight yourself also in the Lord, and He shall give you the desires of your heart. Commit your way to the Lord, trust also in Him, and He shall bring *it* to pass.

God warns us not to focus too much or be surprised by the naysayers, because the longer you stay on course, the more you'll recognize the infestation, for there will be a lot of them. Unfair and unwarranted criticism rooted in jealousy and pure malice will come your way at full speed to try and take you out of the race.

You'll need to understand that the more successful you become, the more the critics will come out of the woodwork to cripple you. The key to overcoming the simple-minded and immature people is not to take it personally. Many times even though it's directed at you, it's not even about you. It's an issue inside of the person that is lashing out and has become a restraint on their ability to advance and reach greater heights. As believers we must rise above the fray and continue to run steadily to the mark that is designed for us. Maintaining the proper attitude is crucial in reaching that plateau arriving at a predictable conclusion. Paul warns the believers to keep their eyes on the prize, stay focused, and be diligent while anticipating the rejection and persecution.

Jesus, when He sent His disciples into the towns, explained to them that they would encounter some grateful people, and some rude and thankless people also, but told them not to allow their attitudes to keep them from their mission and the tasks that lie ahead of them. He instructed His disciples that when they go into the cities and are subjected to rejection to shake the dust off their feet. In other words, keep it moving. Leave the haters and the backbiters to their own devices and continue to achieve their goals in spite of their enemies.

Your purpose is too valuable and important to allow the venom of your enemies to poison you. Don't give the enemies five seconds of your time trying to figure them out. Stay positive and keep it one hundred. Recognize who you are in the Kingdom of God. Their purpose and intentions are to attack you. However, you cannot be stopped or hindered by negative vibes. Recognize that their vicious and scandalous remarks will only add fuel to your tank to motivate you. Build up a resistance against misguided individuals, not giving them the satisfaction of seeing you get off course.

Your duty — or should I say, assignment — is to stay on the track and run your laps with vigor and passion. Keep your head straight and maintain a forward vision with every stride; making leaps and bounds to reaching your goal that gets closer and closer. Don't worry about the bumps and the bruises that you will endure on this road. Many great men have encountered, experienced, and overcome those same obstacles. Ted Turner, who never graduated from high school, went on to found and create the TBS, TNT, and CNN television stations in spite of the bumps and bruises that were poised to keep him out of the race. Albert Einstein flunked out of school and experienced speech difficulties but became a great inventor and physicist. Jim Casey, who founded the UPS Corporation, never graduated but did not allow the lack of a diploma to stop him from achieving and contributing great things.

So I challenge every person that may have fallen, slipped or just given up to get back in your lane and fulfill your destiny. It is not too late to get your second wind, to start right back where you left off. Learn from your mistakes and make this declaration unto yourself: "I am too close to give up now." Your best is yet to come. Successful people do not close shop over one mishap; they go back to the drawing board. You're coming down the home stretch, and while your muscles may be tired and your face may be burning, the truth that remains is that you can see the finish line and it is within reach. So continue to challenge yourself and push yourself because you're almost there. There is too much riding on this race, and it is comprised of the sweat and tears, as well as the scrapes and bruises.

Ridicule and lies, criticism and lonely moments, as well as sleepless nights were all endured along this journey. There are plenty of times that you wanted to throw in the towel and moments when you didn't know whether you'd make it or not, but in spite of all of that, you hung in there running at a brisk, yet steady pace. You understood that it was more than you running the laps; you knew that generations were tied to you completing the course.

Who is willing to finish this race? Paul contends in 2 Timothy 4:6–8:

> For I am already being poured out as a drink offering, and the time of my departure is at hand. I have fought the good fight, I have finished the race, I have kept the faith. Finally, there is laid up for me the crown of righteousness, which the

Lord, the righteous Judge, will give to me on that day, and not to me only but also to all who have loved His appearing.

Like the Apostle Paul, we must stay on course knowing that there's a crown in store for all of us who are willing to finish this race. We must fight an earnest and faithful fight that will enable us to overcome the many obstacles that we'll face on the way to the finish line, conscious of the fact that through Christ, we can do all things.

I challenge each and every one of you to reach the finish line, become all that you can be, live life to the fullest, reach out for the stars, dream big, and never accept failure as an option. Reach down inside of yourself and pull out the champion that resides inside. You're in the home stretch with the wind against your back. Reach I say, reach for the finish line. You've come too far to be denied. You will put failure, fear, and depression and all those ungodly emotions to rest. Start embracing the word "champion" and associate it with your name. Take advantage of the fact that you're in the family of Jesus Christ and all that has been made possible through His blood that which has been shed for us.

Take in this moment, as you are about to cross over the finish line. Reflect on that moment when you wanted to give up. You have received the words sent by God as encouragement, provoking you to continue. Congratulations! You reached the finish line.

QUESTIONS FOR "STRETCHING FOR THE FINISH LINE":

1] What goals did you set in preparation for this journey? Did youreach those goals? Explain.

a] _____
_____
_____
_____

2] How can your journey help propel someone else to prepare to reach their destiny?

a] _____
_____
_____
_____

Epilogue

"Nothing great and durable has ever been produced with ease. Labor is the parent of all the lasting monuments of the world; whether in verse or in stone, in poetry or in pyramids."
Thomas Moore

As you have finished reading this book and filled in your answers to the worksheets at the end of each chapter, I challenge you to find your purpose in life. And after finding your purpose, I challenge you to fulfill your destiny, to tap into all of the resources that are available to you. Become energized and passionate about your future. Embrace every challenge that may come your way and aggressively pursue your dreams, especially those that have been dormant for years.

Look in the mirror and remember the praise that David exclaimed in Psalm 139:14**:** "I will praise You, for I am fearfully *and* wonderfully made;

marvelous are Your works, and *that* my soul knows very well." Begin your process of rediscovering yourself. Dust off the cobwebs that have attached themselves unto you. Shake them off!

Let the words on the pages you've just read serve as the catalyst that propels you to greater heights. Remember that you have the DNA of the Almighty God, which means that you are equipped to do great and mighty things. You are filled with wisdom and strength, talent and creativity, to conquer anything you put your mind to. My hope is that when you close this book that you are inspired, encouraged, and prepared to walk in your destiny.

Find out finally who you were created to be through the words of God and not through the opinions of people, who themselves are also searching for answers. So whether you are standing at a crossroad in your life or just stagnant, this book will help to jump-start your engine again and help you assess valuable information to reach your goals while developing an attitude to win.

So as our time together comes to a conclusion, I pray that you allow God to fill every void in your life, that your personal relationship with God reaches deeper heights, and that the peace of the Lord will surround and comfort you, bringing about peace and fulfillment in your life. Remember that no matter what you have encountered in life before, God still loves you and has given you another day, a chance to go forward and exceed your wildest expectation.

Rise up and stand on the word of God, and know that this is your season to walk the path toward the purpose that the Lord has placed in your life.

References

Brown, J. B., Jr. Quotes.
http://thinkexist.com/quotes/h._jackson_brown,_jr./

Einstein, A.
http://www.biography.com/people/albert-einstein-9285408#early-life&

Holy Bible [NKJV]. http://legacy.Biblegateway.com/

Walker, P. (1983). *Lost in the Cosmos: The Last Self-Help Book.*
   New York, NY. McGraw-Hill

CPSIA information can be obtained at www.ICGtesting.com
Printed in the USA
LVOW06s0043251014

410436LV00001B/4/P